JESSICA KING

From
LOST
DAUGHTER
To
HIDDEN
DAUGHTER

A **SINGLE** WOMAN'S JOURNEY
TOWARDS WHOLENESS
AND PEACE WITHIN

From Lost Daughter to Hidden Daughter
A Single Woman's Journey Towards Wholeness and Peace Within
by Jessica King

©2020, Jessica King

Cover Design:
Anointed Fire

Published by:
Anointed Fire

ISBN: 978-1-7354654-0-1

This book contains material protected under International and Federal Copyright Laws and Treaties. Any unauthorized reprint or use of this material is prohibited. No part of this book may be reproduced or transmitted in any form or by any means, electronic or mechanical, including photocopying, recording, or by any information storage and retrieval system without express written permission from the author/publisher.

Although the author and publisher have made every effort to ensure that the information in this book was correct at press time, the author and publisher do not assume and hereby disclaim any liability to any party for any loss, damage, or disruption caused by errors or omissions, whether such errors or omissions result from negligence, accident, or any other cause.

I have tried to recreate events, locales and conversations from my memories of them. In order to maintain their anonymity in some instances, I have changed the names of individuals and places. I may have changed some identifying characteristics and details such as physical properties, occupations and places of residence.

Although the author and publisher have made every effort to ensure that the information in this book was correct at press time, the author and publisher do not assume and hereby disclaim any liability to any party for any loss, damage, or disruption caused by errors or omissions, whether such errors or omissions result from negligence, accident, or any other cause.

This book is not intended as a substitute for the medical advice of physicians. The reader should regularly consult a physician in matters relating to his/her health and particularly with respect to any symptoms that may require diagnosis or medical attention.

Disclaimer: I am not a psychologist, therapist, theologian, or a deliverance minister. I'm just a hidden daughter who wants to tell you my personal story on how I found wholeness in Christ Jesus. I don't claim that this book will be a magic pill that will stop the pain and bleeding. My purpose is to uplift the sisters. As a man, you will gain little from this book. I hope this book can be the introduction that spars the beginning of your unique journey back to your authentic self.

Additional Note: I have changed the names in this book for privacy measures.

All scriptures noted in this book were taken from ESV, NIV, and KJV, NKJV, Berean, unless otherwise noted.

Acknowledgments:
To ALL my spiritual fathers and mothers who impacted and changed my life.

Special Acknowledgments:
Tiffany Buckner, my spiritual mother who encouraged me to write this book.

Table of Contents

Preface..IX

Prologue...XI

   The Heartbreak that Began my Journey...........XI

Chapter 1..

   An Unsurrendered Life.....................1

Chapter 2..

   The Generational Curse of Shame and Reproach........................9

Chapter 3..

   An Introduction to Coping Mechanisms and Toxic Mindsets..............................51

Chapter 4..

   The Obsession for Romantic Love & Satanic Agenda of a Fatherless Generation...............65

Chapter 5..

   Broken Perception, Insecurity, and the World's Scale...91

Chapter 6..

   The Former Seductress Learns How to Guard Her Heart.....................105

Chapter 7..

   Building Your Own Self-Worth and the Three Virgins......................................123

Chapter 8..........
    Attraction in the Kingdom Language............141

Chapter 9..........
    Lust of the Flesh, Lust of the Eyes, and the Pride of Life................153

Chapter 10..........
    The Product of Trauma is an Adulterous Woman................171

Chapter 11..........
    Unrequited Love and the Samaritan Woman 183

Chapter 12..........
    The Power of Esther and Ruth, God's Ordained Spouse for You 207

Chapter 13..........
    After Healing: The Proverbs 31 Woman......233

Bibliography............CCXLI

About the Author.................CCXLVI

PREFACE

When Jesus lived on Earth, He performed many miracles. These miracles altered the hearts, minds, and lives of the people He encountered. Oxford Languages define miracle as: "an extraordinary and welcome event that is not explicable by natural or scientific laws and is therefore attributed to a divine agency." Miracles can only happen in circumstances, situations, or events that desperately need a positive upturn. Miracles aren't needed when life is easy and smooth sailing. The Bible tells of a woman with the issue of blood.

> **Luke 8:43-48:** And a woman having an issue of blood twelve years, which had spent all her living upon physicians, neither could be healed of any, came behind him, and touched the border of his garment: and immediately her issue of blood stanched. And Jesus said, Who touched me? When all denied, Peter and they that were with him said, Master, the multitude throng thee and press thee, and sayest thou, Who

touched me? And Jesus said, Somebody hath touched me: for I perceive that virtue is gone out of me. And when the woman saw that she was not hid, she came trembling, and falling down before him, she declared unto him before all the people for what cause she had touched him, and how she was healed immediately. And he said unto her, Daughter, be of good comfort: thy faith hath made thee whole; go in peace (KJV).

The woman who had been bleeding for 12 years represents me, except I had been bleeding for the past 25 years of my life. That is until Jesus touched, delivered, and set me free. I imagined the woman with the issue of blood crawling through the crowd on her knees and shoving all the people aside. She was not ashamed about what she looked like to others. In spite of the blood that trailed behind her, she pushed and moved along. This woman was desperate for freedom. In order to receive deliverance and healing, one must humble themselves before the Lord. To be humble means to feel like a fool. I had felt like a fool many times during this long journey of restoration.

PROLOGUE

The Heartbreak that Began my Journey

May 10, 2017. I had carefully written that date in my black moleskin journal. "The day my heart shattered" were the words I scribbled inside. In my head, I had envisioned that I would walk down the aisle with the *man I 'loved.'* My romantic fantasy consisted of moving to his home country, supporting him as his helpmeet, and rearing God-fearing children *together*. Little did I know on May 10, 2017, God had different plans for our individual lives.

May 10, 2017 was when he agreed to meet me at a local hamburger joint near the university I attended. I prepared a little journal wrapped in plastic. On a random given day, the Lord had prompted me to enter a local art shop. A little push in my spirit directed me to buy a gift for the *man I 'loved.'* In my mind, it would end up like a fairy tale. I would parade myself in front of him, present him the little journal, and confess my feelings to him. After all, this is what I learned from the Korean soap operas that consumed my mind. He would then respond in pleasant surprise. We would forever parade together in the sunset.

I had prostrated myself before the Lord, and I prayed for an entire year for *this man*. I also had secretly crushed on him for the past three years during my collegiate career. That previous year, I begged, pleaded, and whined in the presence of our heavenly Father. This *man I loved* and I had been separated for more than a year because he was studying abroad in his motherland. In my mind, this was a Korean soap opera in the making.

Korean soap operas were my stronghold. In Korean dramas, a beautiful damsel in distress meets her handsome gentleman who essentially is Jesus in handsome flesh. He metaphorically rescues the damsel in distress and they end up living happily ever after. Unfortunately, I was in for a hard, cold and brutal awakening called reality.

I remember the moment clearly. I came ten minutes early to our agreed designated spot. I sat at a random seat by the window. My older sister in the faith at the time had suggested that I ask him out on a lunch date to confirm his relational status. Secretly, I already knew he had a girlfriend. God tried to tell me two times through two friends, but I was too entrenched in my fantasies to take heed to their warning. Although she had emphasized that this was for confirmation purposes only, I had already planned the wedding in my head. I firmly believed in the *'fact'* that God had told me that the *man I loved* was my husband.

The color from my face drained when he did not show up after I waited for ten whole minutes. Ten minutes turned to twenty. Twenty turned to thirty. Eventually, he did show up very late, yet, I was excited. After all, the *man I loved* was going to accept my proposition. Instead, I didn't get a chance to speak. He saw the expression on my face and said flatly, "I have a girlfriend."

I tried to compose myself. "This couldn't be true," I thought to myself. The conversation was brief. He got up and excused himself for a moment. I desperately tried to hold back all my disbelief. I had to come to a point of decision amidst confusion.

Would I give him the gift despite not being able to confess my feelings?

My obsession for him ran deep to the

core, but in the end, I chose to treat him as a brother in Christ. He had confessed that he was seeing a nonbeliever. His depression was spiraling out of control. I gave him that little journal, and he thanked me profusely because he really needed it. Unfortunately, I also left him a piece of my heart in that little journal, with the hope that God would reunite us one day in the future when we would both mature in the Lord. After all, I believed that the best ending was when two lovebirds reunite after an earth-long separation. After three years, I was finally able to let him fully go when I grieved my childhood, the loss of my friendship with him, and the dreams I formed in my head regarding him.

These were dreams that I unintentionally tied to the *man I loved*. God also spoke to me that the best and most romantic ending is where He gets the most glory.

In the end, God's plans triumphed over mine. This wasn't the first man I'd 'loved.' I had a track record of one-sided emotional soul ties that stemmed all the way back to elementary school.

Hosea 6:1: Come, let us return to the Lord. For He has torn us, but He will heal us; He has wounded us, but He will bandage us (NASB).

God had to break me and strip me of my idols in order to heal my heart. Just like the Israelites who had various obsessions, I also had mine. Although my idols didn't come in the form of golden states, my obsessions displeased God just as much. My obsessions came in nicely wrapped flesh and toxic mindsets.

To begin my healing journey, God used the *man I loved as an instrument.* He was one of the many men I had lusted after since kindergarten. Like an onion, God peeled away one rotting layer at a time until He was able to get to the core—my unresolved grief that originated from my tumultuous childhood. He took me through a three-year wilderness journey with Him before He gave me back my peace.

Chapter 1

An Unsurrendered Life

Healing happens in layers. Often, it takes an immediate situation in one's present circumstance to wake that person up to the harshness of a brutal reality. In an ideal world, the root of an issue would be first dealt with. Therefore, bad fruit that results from bad roots would cease to grow.

When I turned 18, I became a Christ-follower. Unfortunately, I was unable to bear the fruits of the Spirit that my other Christian peers experienced, because the root of my pain was not cut down. Love, joy, peace, patience, kindness, goodness, faithfulness, gentleness, and self-control seemed to escape me (Galatians 5:22-5:23). Instead, I bore rotten fruits that I hid from the public, because I feared rejection from my peers. The fear of rejection kept my own sins in the dark, which resulted in my sin festering like mold in humid climates.

Unfortunately, we don't live in an ideal world. God often has to deal with the immediate issue at hand before cutting down the root. He had to cut down the bad fruit that resulted from my idolatry by separating me from a toxic, one-sided emotional soul tie.

Soul ties are formed through our mind, will, and emotions. The Bible tells women, "Above all else, guard your heart, for everything you do flows from it" (Proverbs 4:23, NIV). The word heart in Hebrew is *leb*, which means inner man. Human beings are comprised of two components: the outer man and the inner man. The outer man is our flesh, whereas, the inner man is where our soul resides. Our soul is the epicenter of our mind, will, and emotions. In the Bible, David and Jonathan are an example of a soul tie. Saul was after the life of King David, yet Saul's son, Jonathan, developed a close kinship with David. These two were placed together during a specific season for a specific purpose. Jonathan was in David's life to help him escape from Saul.

1 Samuel 18:1 As soon as he had finished speaking to Saul, the **soul** of Jonathan was **knit** to the **soul** of David, and Jonathan loved him as his own soul (ESV).

When I was a campus missionary in East Asia, my co-laborer, Bethany and I had developed a soul tie. We sacrificed, loved, fought, and cared for one another like we were blood-related relatives. During that time, God often put me in positions where I was her Aaron, and she was my Moses. Aaron often spoke on behalf of Moses, because Moses had some insecurities regarding his speech. Although it was imperfect, God was the one who knitted our souls together. There was favor found in our friendship. In fact, when God called Bethany out of the field, I felt a piece of my soul break off. I grieved the separation of a close sister and friend.

As I mentioned previously, at that time, I firmly believed that the love I had for the *man I loved* was genuine, unadulterated, and pure. The reality of the situation was that particular *man I loved triggered* the spirit of obsession within me. I was willing to forego my truest identity to gain a morsel of *'love'* from him. I desired to move to his motherland and chase after him, because I thought following this man would create eternal happiness within me. The reason why I had become so obsessed with this man was because I created a fantasy world to numb the deep pain inside of me. This man and the idea of creating a future with him became the source of my deepest joy. In essence, he was simply one of the many band-aids that I used as an attempt to cease the internal bleeding from my childhood wounds. Unlike Bethany, *the man I loved* was simply a demonic soul tie.

Demonic soul ties work in a similar fashion, except demonic soul ties are formed by the hands of the enemy. The purpose of demonic soul ties is to kill, steal, and destroy a believer's call and purpose (John 10:10). Often, Satan uses our romantic choices against us so that we may choose the counterfeit (Ishmael) rather than waiting for our promise (Isaac). When God promised Abram that he would be a father of many nations, the promise was meant to come through Isaac. Sarah had to wait on God's timing to fulfill His promise for them. Instead, she grew impatient, and she laughed at God's promise for her. The result was detrimental, as she demanded that her husband sleep with her maid, Hagar. It is impossible to please God without faith. As a result, Ishmael was born. Arguably speaking, God can redeem many of our poor choices, but it is best to seek God for His good, perfect, and pleasing will (Romans 12:2). Unfortunately, many believers end up settling for their Ishmael when God has their Isaac just around the corner. This frequently happens when we are young and have not fully submitted and surrendered our lives to the Lord. Due to our traumatic childhoods, we developed trust issues and put people and God at arm's distance. This manifests when we only allow God in certain areas of our lives, all the while, demanding control in other areas.

As an example, when I first became a believer, I had my own plans for my life. Growing up in a loveless home, instead of developing a sense of who I was and my own boundaries, I spent the majority of my childhood appeasing the emotional needs and voids of my parental units. As a young woman, my life's pursuits stemmed from the deep emotional void that originated in childhood. In essence, the spirit of rejection entered in my mother's womb. Rejection followed me around like my own shadow. My fantasies consisted of becoming a world-renowned singer. I wanted to be worshipped, loved, and admired. Due to my father's unresolved self-hatred, he not only sexually abused me, but also negatively commented on my physical features. I grew up believing I was the ugliest girl in the world. I was one of the few ethnic minorities in my neighborhood and school, so I could not fit in anywhere. I also didn't have blonde hair or blue eyes like the majority of my peers, so I deemed myself to be ugly. When I discovered the world of K-pop (Korean popular music), a false hope developed, because I saw that women of Asian descent could be called beautiful and desired by men. It appeared that there was a beauty standard that I could religiously follow. If I followed suit, I would finally become 'beautiful.' Instead of seeking the Lord's will for my life, I sought after the notion of being loved, worshipped, and admired by others to ease the void of being rejected by my own father.

K-pop (Korean popular music) is the Asian equivalent of the American hip-hop and rap culture. Just like many youths in America garner their identity and value in what is known as hip-hop and rap culture, lost youths of Asian descent often form communities revolving around their love for K-pop. Unlike the American music industry, a mixtape or EP is not required to enter the major companies in Korea that train potential singers and entertainers. In K-pop, talent is essentially not required, but a certain look was essential for success in the market. This certain look was the key to enter in one of the major entertainment companies, thereby, being trained to potentially debut as a musician or in a girl group.

    Beginning in middle school, I began to submit online audition tapes to the three major entertainment companies in Korea. My biggest dream at the time was to enter in one of the major entertainment companies in Korea. I wanted to become a trainee, one who trains for several years in singing, dancing, acting, and languages.

    For me, I yearned to become a singer so that people would love and notice me. By the grace of God, He closed these doors, so my already broken soul would not be further shattered into a million pieces. When I turned 18 and became a Christian, I had not fully surrendered these dreams. K-pop Star, the Korean equivalent of The Voice, came to my hometown during the summer of the first year I came back home from college. At the time, I was growing weary of holding on to a fruitless dream. I told God that if I didn't pass this audition, I would give up on becoming a K-pop star. I didn't pass, and therefore, I surrendered my dream to God.

    The lengthy example that I illustrated above is just one of the many times as a young woman when I allowed myself to steer the steering wheel of my life. Idolatry runs in my bloodline, and I often became obsessed with the dreams I had planned for myself. Later on, God taught me how to turn that obsession into obsession for Jesus, His Son. I also learned to find myself beautiful and to see myself through the eyes of my Maker.

Chapter 2

The Generational Curse of Shame and Reproach

Proverbs 4:23: *Keep your heart with all vigilance, for from it flow the springs of life (ESV).*

According to Merriam-Webster, to guard means to "watch over so as to prevent escape, disclosure, or discretion." The word heart is synonymous to the word life. Everything flows from our heart (life). The momentum flow is similar to the motion that bodies of water make. The body of water called the river has an origin, and this origin is called its source. Our hearts are the source of our lives. Metaphorically speaking, this is where the river begins. If we take this a little deeper, other translations state, "Carefully guard your thoughts because they are the source of true life" (CEV) and "Be careful how you think; your life is shaped by your thoughts" (GNT). This leads me to conclude that the heart and the mind are interconnected. "For as he thinketh in his heart, so is he" is a verse found in Proverbs 23:7 (KJV). It appears to be that what we chose to think and meditate on eventually flows and sinks into our hearts. This becomes the source of who we are.

    Unfortunately, when a young girl is sexually abused, raped, molested, beat, emotionally manipulated, or forced to become a surrogate wife, just to name a few tragedies that occur in this world, the young girl grows up to become a brokenhearted woman. This brokenhearted woman has unprocessed grief, anger, bitterness, and resentment. She holds back all the years of abuse and neglect under the guise of her own pretentiousness. The brutal truth is the dam of her neglect that has been held under by her own strength will eventually breakdown under the pressures of life. When the pressure of life storms in and eventually breaks her carefully constructed dam, she will be forced to face the reality of her past. She will eventually outrun herself, and out of necessity, will run into herself to face her demons.

The Generational Curse of Shame and Reproach

The grown brokenhearted woman subconsciously identifies herself based on her abuse. She often thinks that she is a sexual object and worth nothing more than her body. This is what she consciously fights to do in the natural, yet, she often fails to exhibit the confidence to do so. The deep shame and reproach that she carries only serves to suffocate her. This reproach is the same disgrace that Tamar felt when her half-brother, Amnon, raped her. Any form of unwanted sexual contact by an adult to a child creates a deep-seated shame. This shame runs deep to her core down to her inner man.

Tamar tells Amnon after her rape,
> "As for me, where could I get rid of my **reproach**? And as for you, you will be like one of the fools in Israel. Now therefore, please speak to the king, for he will not withhold me from you" (2 Samuel 13:13, NASB).

The word reproach is Hebrew for *cherpah.* Reproach rests upon the condition of shame and disgrace (Blue Letter Bible). The atrocious and horrific act that Ammon committed leads to Tamar's grief. It appears that she cannot shake her reproach or, in other words, her deep-seated shame.

> **2 Samuel 13:19:** Tamar put **ashes** on her head and tore her long-sleeved garment which was on her; and she put her hand on her head and went away, crying aloud as she went (NASB).

In the Bible, ashes often symbolize grief (Isaiah 61:3), humiliation, or penitence (the act of feeling or showing sorrow and regret for having done wrong). To cover with ashes represented self-abhorrence (a feeling of disgusted loathing or revulsion and humiliation) (Reference: Oxford Languages/ Bible Study Tools). In conclusion, Tamar wept bitterly because she felt humiliation, sorrow, and regret. She felt disgusted and penitent over an injustice committed to her. It **WAS NOT** her fault. She was a victim of a crime perpetrated by her half-brother, and she was left alone to carry all the intense emotions of loathing and revulsion. "To be shame-bound means that whenever you feel any feeling, need or drive, you immediately feel ashamed. The dynamic core of your human life is grounded in your feelings, needs, and drives. When these are bound by shame, you are shamed to the core" (Reference: John Bradshaw, Healing the Shame that Binds You).

Unfortunately, in many cases, sexual abuse victims, especially young women, end up internalizing the humiliation, sorrow, regret, disgust, loathing, revulsion, and disgrace. These survivors walk around this world for many years with a fragmented soul. The perpetrator takes a part of the young girl's soul through the sexual act, even if the sexual act doesn't result in penetration. As an example, when my father sexually abused me, he broke off a piece of my soul (mind, will, and emotions).

When I was seven years old, my biological father began to sexually abuse me. My entire world was shattered forever when my biological father aggressively grabbed my hand to rub against his reproductive organ. The sexual abuse was an off-and-on occurrence; it finally ended when I was around 12 years old. I learned that I was not physically strong enough to fight back his advances, and eventually, I quit fighting as intensely.

Before the manifestation of the sexual act, my entire family structure was out of order and not formed by God's original design. My father was a little boy in the outward covering of a grown man. Despite being 17 years my mother's senior, he struggled profusely with self-control. He had a spending problem. By the time I turned 7, there were decorations galore encompassing my entire house. He spent over the family's income on paintings, furniture, clothes, and other name brand items. He seemed to care more about the external presentation of the family than the internal state. Later, I found out he borrowed money from my mother's credit cards. I spent my youth hearing the debt collectors call my house day in and day out.

My father is a classic example of self-made rags to riches, turned into riches to rags man. Due to his uncontrollable appetite and lusts, he spent the majority of the fortune he earned. By the time I turned 7, my mother took on a job at a local Chinese restaurant to support her three children: my father, my brother, and I.

All these facts aside, my mother and father's marriage was built on a rocky foundation to begin with. China was an impoverished country during my mother's generation. My grandparents on my mother's side were factory workers. If I remember correctly, my mother mentioned that she used ration coupons to buy fruits. It was rare to eat an orange or a banana back in the day. A woman getting a college education in my mother's generation was a rare commodity. My mother's sister, my aunt, was the brain of the house, and she went to college. My mother enjoyed doing housework, and she didn't like to study. With a middle to high school education, the opportunities were limited for her. My mother was pressured into marriage by her mother, my grandmother. She was constantly forced on blind dates. Sometimes, she would purposely wander the streets after leaving ten minutes from a date, because she didn't like the young man. She arrived home hours later so she would not face her mother yelling at her for rejecting another potential suitor.

Later, she met her husband at work; her boss became her husband. My grandparents didn't like my father. For the engagement/bridal gift, my father was stingy despite being wealthy at the time. My mother didn't heed to her parents' warning. A young woman at the time, she immigrated to the USA with my father in 1991. I was born in 1995 in Houston, Texas. On the outside, it appeared that their marriage was a match made in heaven. They were physically attractive, and they lived in a beautiful home. At a quick first glance, the American dream became their reality. The truth of the matter was that my father, a businessman, had wanderlust and was rarely home. Before I turned 7, I don't remember much of my father.

One profound memory that sticks close to me happened when I was between three to five years old. By this time, my father had been gone for a significantly long period of time. My mother was furious. She commanded my younger brother and I to go to the study room and aid her in ripping apart all his certificates and other important documents. At the time, I wasn't aware that their marital issues had occurred before then, because they slept in different rooms. This vivid memory shaped my perspective that my parents were not on good terms.

Leviticus 18 is an entire chapter dedicated to describing unlawful sexual relations. Leviticus 18:23 states, "Do not have sexual relations with an animal and defile yourself with it. A woman must not present herself to an animal to have sexual relations with it; that is a perversion" (NIV). This is just an example of how corrupt the world had become during the Old Testament times. This kind of law had to be written because the people of God were becoming more perverse, deviating from God's original intent. The reality is that because of the world that we live in, perversion will always be present.

Below are some statistics on child abuse that occurs in modern times.
- 1 out of 3 girls and 1 out of 5 boys will be sexually abused before they reach age 18.
- 90% of child sexual abuse victims know the perpetrator in some way. 68% are abused by a family member.
- In 2012, 82.2% of child abuse perpetrators were found to be between

the ages of 18-44, of which 39.6% were recorded to be between the ages of 25-34.
- In the United States, more than 4 children die from child abuse and neglect on a daily basis. Over 70% of these children are below the age of 3.
- Boys (48.5%) and girls (51.2%) become victims at nearly the same rate.
- 2.9 million cases of child abuse are reported every year in the United States.
- Children who experience child abuse and neglect are 59% more likely to be arrested as a juvenile, 28% more likely to be arrested as an adult, and 30% more likely to commit violence crime.
- About 80% of 21-year-olds who were abused as children met criteria for at least one psychological disorder.
- 14% of all men and 36% of all women in prison were abused as children.
- Abused children are less likely to practice safe sex, putting them at greater risk for STDs. They're also 25% more likely to experience teen pregnancy.

(Reference: Do Something / 11 Facts about Child Abuse)

The Generational Curse of Shame and Reproach

The victims of child abuse are victims of trauma. Trauma refers to an emotional response to a terrible event (Reference: American Psychological Association/ Trauma and Shock). It often causes people to live in denial of the terrible event that occurred in their lives. In my case, I was in denial about my childhood trauma for the majority of my life. In my family, the foundation for love was never set in place. Trauma is often generational. In the spiritual world, it is referred to as generational curses. A generational curse is when ones' ancestors commit an injustice towards another person and/or group of people. The consequences of the committed sin pass down to the next generation. A simple example of this in my life is that my great grandmother on my father's side was a Manchurian woman. In ancient times, Manchurians were guilty of bloodshed, because they utterly destroyed an entire clan of Mongolian men, women, and children. The Manchurians also built a monument following their upheaval. This created a curse that was passed down to me from the third and fourth generation. I had to pray, renounce, disassociate myself from their crimes and declare that I am God's child only.

The Generational Curse of Shame and Reproach

Numbers 14:18: The Lord is slow to anger and abounding in steadfast love, forgiving iniquity and transgression, but <u>he will by no means clear the guilty, visiting the iniquity of the fathers on the children, to the third and the fourth generation</u> (ESV).

 My parents had come from traumatic backgrounds themselves, so they were unable to be whole and completely available for their own children. My father grew up in China during the Cultural Revolution. This was an event in history where the peasant class revolted against the intellectuals. My grandfather was a high-ranking government official. Therefore, the entire family experienced cruelty and injustices such as defamation and vandalism. My father's sister detailed her experience of injustice, such as when the peasant class threw chili sauce on their home. She remembers my grandmother walking on the streets and having rocks thrown at her as well. My grandmother was a devout, but hidden, Buddhist. She hid her religion for safety precautions.

The Generational Curse of Shame and Reproach

The Cultural Revolution is better known as the 'A Scar on the Chinese Soul.' The New York Times states:

"The psychic damage of the Cultural Revolution has been the subject of only a few small-scale studies. An interview project carried out by Chinese researchers in collaboration with German psychotherapists in the early 2000s showed that people with Cultural Revolution-related trauma exhibited symptoms typical of post-traumatic stress disorder: Many reported intense anxiety, depression and frequent flashbacks of traumatic experiences; some showed emotional numbness and avoidance behaviors.

Cultural Revolution trauma differs from that related to other horrific events, like the Holocaust and the Rwandan genocide, studies have noted, in part because in China, people were persecuted not for "unalterable" characteristics such as ethnicity and race, but for having the wrong frame of mind. Constant scrutiny of one's own thinking and actions for signs of political deviance became a necessity for survival that sometimes carried unbearable weight" (A Scar on The Chinese Soul).

My father, who grew up during a period of social unrest, was brought up in an environment where there was an inconsistent amount of discipline. He was a gifted writer, musician, and artist. My grandfather was very popular with women due to his political status. Before the revolution occurred, he often took my father to large banquets. My father was made to feel like he was royalty. His mother tried to enact discipline by enforcing stricter rules. This, however, backfired because of the inconsistent style of parenting. When his sister was born, his role as the golden child was taken away, and he became the black sheep. As a young man, an officer of higher rank sexually abused my father when he enrolled in the Chinese military.

The purpose in which I share this long-winded historical account is to illustrate the point that trauma is generational. Epigenetic trauma is when environmental factors influence the expression or suppression of genes (Reference: Pubmed/ Cultural Trauma and Epigenetic Inheritance). There is a strong correlation that war, famine, genocide, civil unrest, and other historical injustices can alter one's DNA. If possible, it is important to trace our family's history to better understand how the past shapes our present, so history does not repeat itself.

My father who had his golden child role stripped away from him decided to raise his own children under the same toxic system. I was worshipped and adored, simply because I was the first-born child. My younger brother, on the other hand, was often abused, humiliated, and belittled by him because he was second-born. Essentially, my father reenacted his childhood by recreating the roles demonstrated to him.

In narcissistic family systems, there are many kinds of dysfunctional roles played. The main roles that I will discuss today are the scapegoat and the golden child. The scapegoat is essentially the family's human trashcan. All the disappointment, anger, and internalized hatred that the narcissist feels would thereby be placed on the scapegoat. The golden child is worshipped and often placed in an unwanted role of a surrogate spouse. When my mother left for work to support the family, I spent a lot of time with my brother and father. One time, when I was sitting on the couch, my father confided in me that his sex life with my mother was nonexistent. A young child should NOT bear this emotional burden. This was the epitome of trauma.

The Bible also demonstrates this concept of favoritism. Isaac and Rebecca's children grew up in a dysfunctional environment. Isaac favored Esau, whereas Rebecca favored Isaac.

> **Genesis 25:28:** Isaac, who had a taste for wild game, loved Esau, but Rebekah loved Jacob (NIV).

Isaac identified and easily got along with Esau who was similar to his nature. Esau was described as "a skillful hunter, a man of the open country," while Jacob was "content at home among the tents" (Genesis 25:27, NIV). Isaac, an outdoorsman, carnally gravitated to his son who loved to hunt and kill wild animals, while Rebecca doted on Jacob who stayed at home by her side. Perhaps, Rebecca identified more with Jacob's spirit. The sin of favoritism created an unhealthy family dynamic. This, in turn, created even further animosity and division between the two blood-related brothers. Unfortunately, Jacob's unrepentant sin of favoritism encroached his decision-making skills. Instead of seeking the will of God, he chose his future mate based on what pleased his flesh.

> **Genesis 29:16-17:** Now Laban had two daughters; the name of the older was Leah, and the name of the younger was Rachel. Leah had **weak eyes**, but Rachel had a **lovely figure** and was **beautiful** (NIV).

When he laid his eyes on Rachel for the first time, he did not introduce himself; instead, he immediately greeted her with a kiss. It was a custom during those times to greet people with kisses. Rachel must have been taken aback by the sudden greeting of an unnamed stranger who later wept aloud. After his loud weeping, he finally introduces himself. Rachel runs home to tell her father about a relative that has come to visit her. In biblical days, it was the father's role to determine when the daughter was ready for marriage and whom she should be betrothed to. The bridegroom gave a dowry or *mohar* to the bride's father in exchange for her hand in marriage. Jacob felt "an intense feeling of romantic attachment based on an attraction felt by himself for Rachel (Oxford Languages). Laban, Rachel's father, agrees to allow Jacob to become Rachel's bridegroom on the condition that Jacob works for seven years.

In the end, Jacob's favoritism set a foundation for a poor marriage, and therefore, a poor family structure. He essentially lusts after Rachel. Perhaps, Laban sensed Jacob's lust for his daughter and deemed him a poor choice as a suitor. Perhaps, Laban delayed giving Rachel to Jacob because he wanted to test Jacob's character to see if he was worthy of his youngest daughter. Jacob, upon being tricked by Laban, first consummates with Leah. After working for seven more years, he consummates with Rachel. Throughout the marriage, Jacob clearly favors Rachel.

>**Genesis 29:32:** Leah became pregnant and gave birth to a son. She named him **Reuben**, for she said, "It is because the

LORD has seen my misery. Surely my husband will love me now" (NIV).

Genesis 29:33: She conceived again, and when she gave birth to a son she said, "Because the LORD heard that I am not loved, he gave me this one too." So she named him **Simeon** (NIV).

Genesis 29:34: Again she conceived, and when she gave birth to a son she said, "Now at last my husband will become attached to me, because I have borne him three sons." So he was named **Levi** (NIV).

Genesis 29:35: She conceived again, and when she gave birth to a son she said, "This time I will praise the LORD." So she named him **Judah**. Then she stopped having children (NIV).

It is clear that Leah felt unloved and rejected by her own husband. Therefore, the spirit of rejection entered into her womb. She essentially named her first three sons from a spirit of self-loathing. An unhealthy marital covenant leads to unhealthy dynamics between sibling relationships. One of Joseph's unnamed siblings passionately despised him. Noted below, "When Joseph's brothers saw him coming, they recognized him in the distance. As he approached, they made plans to kill him. 'Here comes the dreamer!' they said. 'Come on, let's kill him and throw him into one of these cisterns. We can tell our father, 'A wild animal has eaten him.' Then we'll see what becomes of his dreams!'" (Genesis 37:18-20).

Without love, there is division. A house divided cannot stand. In my family of origin, due to my father's unhealthy favoritism towards me, my brother and I were often found at odds against one another. Psychology Today writes, "When parenting is toxic, such as when it's overly strict or abusive, the perpetrator often vents his or her rage on the younger sibling" (Reference: Sibling Bullying and Abuse: The Hidden Epidemic). Growing up, I was a violent little girl and I would aggressively punch my brother until his nose bled. The toxic favoritism my father had towards me led my own mother to display feelings of jealousy against me. As a child, I felt unloved by my own mother. I could see hatred in her eyes and annoyance that seeped out in her tone and mannerisms towards me. She had a preference over my brother, because she felt like I was her competition towards the affections of my father. Once, she kicked me in the face when I had attempted to dunk my brother's head in our backyard's pond. Just like my father firmly believed that his mother had a preference for his sister over him, I too had the same feelings towards my own mother. In turn, my father's unresolved trauma trickled down to the next generation. Illustrated above is a glimpse of my family's dysfunction, and my own sin that played out in my role as a golden child.

    The Bible emphasizes the importance of the head of the home. The husband plays this crucial role. He is the wife's covering. When the husband does not fulfill his role, this creates a domino effect which causes the whole family's system to fall apart. A father who does not protect, provide, and lead his family garners disrespect. The wife, in turn, has to take on the role of a husband. The wife has a carnal love for her children. Even if she does not display mature love, she still feels a strong sense of responsibility for what has come out of her own womb. Naturally, she then would have to take on a job to support her family if the husband proves negligent in his role.

    While my mother took on the paternal role, my father took on the maternal role. As I grew older, I did not resonate with my peers who wanted to be mothers. I absolutely despised the idea of becoming a mother, because I had unresolved resentment towards her. My mother failed to be nurturing or caring. There is often this unspoken taboo against being honest about our mothers' imperfections. After all, our mothers are the ones who sacrificed for us in many different ways. In my home, my mother sacrificed her comfortable life in order to take a job as a waitress. As I witnessed the evident sacrifices my mother made, the excuses that I made for her behavior were the excuses that I would not give for my father. Yet, I stunted my own healing journey when I failed to acknowledge the extent of hurt that my mother left me. John Bradshaw writes: "To truly be committed to a life of honesty, love and discipline, we must be willing to commit ourselves to reality" (Healing the Shame that Binds You). In Asian cultures, there is a toxic honor system, loyalty at the expense of self. To truly honor thy mother and father, we must first acknowledge the extent and harm that was inflicted upon us. Before my mother took on a full-time job at a local Chinese restaurant, she was mentally unstable. Objectively speaking, she did not speak the language, plus, the loneliness of living in a foreign country without friends took a mental toll on her. Nonetheless, this did not excuse the extent of harm that she contributed to my developing years. I still remember vividly when my mother lay on her bed silent and motionless. This was around the time when I was between three to five years old. I had screamed and pleaded for her to wake up. There was not one sound or movement. Eventually, she did wake up, and she told me that she was the golden statue and if I ever misbehaved, she would never wake up again. My mother also found it entertaining when she hid from me in the home while I would scream and cry, desperate to find where she was. I firmly believe that demons exist, because there is not any better, logical explanation about why my parents behaved the way they did.

Although I grew up in a relatively nice neighborhood, my family was actually struggling financially. I like to compare suburbia America to an illusion of happiness. Oh, the irony when immigrants leave their home countries to take a shot at life in the USA, only to find out that reality is a hard block to shallow. On the outside of a typical American neighborhood, all the homes look identical. It appears that the Joneses are doing well with their chipper, "How are you?" or "I'm doing just lovely!" The truth of the matter is that we don't know what happens behind each closed door.

On the outside, we appeared normal. We lived in a two-story home, and we even had a piano. The truth of the matter was my parents owed up to tens of thousands of dollars in debt, and in the end, we would lose our home to foreclosure. When my father lost his wealth due to his insatiable lust, our family's economic situation took a downturn. I grew up wearing hand-me-downs from my cousins, eating ramen noodles, and eventually getting free lunch from school. With the help of food stamps, my mom was able to get my brother and I more nutritious meals. In the case above, a financially tumultuous environment was formed, which deepened the effects of trauma.

Trauma manifested in my life through different ways. I became a jealous, competitive, and perfectionistic person. I performed well in academics for the very goal of escaping my financially impoverished situation. My mother valued education and pushed me to do my very best. She taught me to never rely on a man, and I will always thank her for that, because I am who I am because of her. (Unfortunately, I did fall short, and I ended up becoming emotionally dependent on many men). Sometimes, my mom was a tiger mom, and it was *too* much. I feared going home with anything below a C. My peers in elementary school had lives that were different from mine. I wanted desperately to fit in with the popular girls who came from wealthy backgrounds and had nice sets of clothes. I didn't have the opportunity to develop into who I was because of the trauma that I was enduring at home. As a result, I became a chameleon, blending into whatever environment I came in contact with.

Trauma survivors manifest through four defense mechanisms or responses: freeze (dissociative), flight (obsessive/compulsive), fawn (codependent), and fight (narcissistic). Pete Walker's book "Complex PTSD: From

Surviving To Thriving" illustrates this concept. Fight manifests through aggression and outbursts of anger. Flight manifests through perfectionistic, workaholic tendencies with anxiety-ridden thoughts. Fawn manifests through people-pleasing, passivity, low self-esteem, and unhealthy boundaries. Freeze manifests in distrust and solitude. Disassociation is common in freeze such as maladaptive daydreaming (Reference: Pete Walker/ The 4Fs: A Trauma Typology in Complex PTSD).

By far, the biggest manifestation of my trauma came through freezing. I escaped into my mind in order to cope with being sexually abused as a child. The sexual abuse first started when I pushed the wrong door. Satan desired to pervert me at a young age in order to take away my purity. One day, I had watched the wrong TV show in the morning before school started. It was an inappropriate pornographic cartoon. I want to emphasize that it was **NOT** my fault that I watched the cartoon, but it demonstrated the many tactics the enemy would use to kill, steal, or destroy a young life. Instead of educating me about what

The Generational Curse of Shame and Reproach

was wrong with the cartoon, my mother just looked at me with disgust and told my father.

> **Genesis 1:** In the beginning, God created the heavens and the earth. The earth was without form and void, and darkness was over the face of the deep. And the Spirit of God was hovering over the face of the waters.
>
> And God said, "Let there be light," and there was light. And God saw that the light was good. And God separated the light from the darkness. God called the light Day, and the darkness he called Night. And there was evening and there was morning, the first day.
>
> And God said, "Let there be an expanse in the midst of the waters, and let it separate the waters from the waters." And God made the expanse and separated the waters that were under the expanse from the waters that were above the expanse. And it was so. And God called the expanse Heaven. And there was evening and there was morning, the second day.

And God said, "Let the waters under the heavens be gathered together into one place, and let the dry land appear." And it was so. God called the dry land Earth, and the waters that were gathered together he called Seas. And God saw that it was good.

And God said, "Let the earth sprout vegetation, plants yielding seed, and fruit trees bearing fruit in which is their seed, each according to its kind, on the earth." And it was so. The earth brought forth vegetation, plants yielding seed according to their own kinds, and trees bearing fruit in which is their seed, each according to its kind. And God saw that it was good. And there was evening and there was morning, the third day.

And God said, "Let there be lights in the expanse of the heavens to separate the day from the night. And let them be for signs and for seasons, and for days and years, and let them be lights in the expanse of the heavens to give light upon the earth." And it was so. And God made the two great lights—the greater light to rule the day and the lesser light to rule the night—and the stars. And God set them in the expanse of the heavens to give light on the earth, to rule over the day and over the night, and to separate the light from the darkness. And God saw that it was good. And there was evening and there was morning, the fourth day.

And God said, "Let the waters swarm with swarms of living creatures, and let birds fly above the earth across the expanse of the heavens." So God created the great sea creatures and every living creature that moves, with which the waters swarm, according to their kinds, and every winged bird according to its kind. And God saw that it was good. And God blessed them, saying, "Be fruitful and multiply and fill the waters in the seas, and let birds multiply on the earth." And there was evening and there was morning, the fifth day.

And God said, "Let the earth bring forth living creatures according to their kinds

The Generational Curse of Shame and Reproach

—livestock and creeping things and beasts of the earth according to their kinds." And it was so. And God made the beasts of the earth according to their kinds and the livestock according to their kinds, and everything that creeps on the ground according to its kind. And God saw that it was good.

Then God said, "Let us make man in our image, after our likeness. And let them have dominion over the fish of the sea and over the birds of the heavens and over the livestock and over all the earth and over every creeping thing that creeps on the earth."

So God created man in his own image, in the image of God he created him; male and female he created them.

And God blessed them. And God said to them, "Be fruitful and multiply and fill the earth and subdue it, and have dominion over the fish of the sea and over the birds of the heavens and over every living thing that moves on the earth." And God said, "Behold, I have given you every plant yielding seed that is on the face of all the earth, and every tree with seed in its fruit. You shall have them for food. And to every beast of the earth and to every bird of the heavens and to everything that creeps on the earth, everything that has the breath of life, I have given every green plant for food." And it was so. And God saw everything that he had made, and behold, it was very good. And there was evening and there was morning, the sixth day (ESV).

The God we serve is a God of order. Oxford Languages define order as, "the arrangement or disposition of people or things in relation to each other according to a particular sequence, pattern, or method." The second definition states "an authoritative command or instruction." In brief, God intentionally placed His authority over His creation through a particular sequence, pattern, or method. His hand-print is over His creation. As the creation, we do not have the authority to dictate how the Creator structures His world, just as it would be absurd if a painting were to argue with the artist over how and where it should be hung up. It is equally absurd for us to self-impose our limited understanding of design onto God's original purpose.

Genesis 1 details the creation of the world. Firstly, God creates the heavens and the earth. Then, He creates night and day. After night and day, He creates the waters and the sky. After He creates the sky, He creates the land. After the land, He creates vegetation. After vegetation, He creates signs to mark the seasons, days, and years. Following that, He creates the sun, moon, and the stars. Then God follows up with fish, birds, and then, land animals. Lastly, He creates human beings.

It is evident that God values order. It would not make any logical sense to create humans without first creating earth for the humans to reside in. In comparison, the act of sex in itself is not wicked or bad. Sex is *only* wrong outside of marriage because God designed the act of sex to occur within the confines of covenant. When we choose to fornicate, we are operating outside of God's original intent and design. Unfortunately, after the fall, Satan perverted God's intent of sex. In the world today, we see this manifested through human trafficking, children brides, pornography, masturbation, fornication, homosexuality, lesbianism, bestiality, polygamy, and pedophilia, just to name a few. A further study of unlawful sexual relations can be found in Leviticus 18.

In my family of origin, my father treated me like a surrogate spouse, instead of a daughter. Emotional incest occurred because there were almost nonexistent emotional boundaries between where my father's began and where mine ended. As a result, I did not view my father as an authority figure, but a peer. The emotional incest slowly but surely created a child who had little respect for her father. In other words, "When a parent is best friends with their child, boundary issues *often* occur. Discipline, expectations, and personal responsibility are all impacted by this behavior. Having a confidante who is not capable or ready to handle adult relationships is forcing the child to set aside their social and psychological world for the sake of their parents" (Reference: Psych Central: Emotional Incest: When is Close Too Close?).

The Generational Curse of Shame and Reproach

The clearest memories I have were of the boundaries between my biological father and myself being blurred. I remember freely entering his master bedroom to encounter my father sitting on the toilet. To this day, I still don't understand why I had such free access to his master bedroom. Thereby, one morning, I ran into his master bedroom and I caught him showering. I burst out laughing. I laughed like no tomorrow. I ran outside of the master bedroom, and my father, the narcissist, was humiliated. I don't remember ever being disciplined about how or why I should not see a naked man showering. In my heart, my gut told me it was wrong, but being a seven-year-old child, I didn't completely understand my actions.

All I knew was that I desired to humiliate my father, and I laughed out of embarrassment. From that day forward, my life changed for the worst. I found myself in the bathroom of his master bedroom. My father was in his underwear and he pulled out his reproductive organ for me to see. When I was sick, my father would take care of me. He would give me medicine, so I would find myself in his master bedroom sleeping on the massage chair. My father would eye my chest area when the massage chair turned on, because my chest would move left and right. Aside from the sudden moments, there were moments when my father aggressively forced my hand to come in direct contact with his reproductive organ. One time, when I was studying, he reached down to touch my breast and said I had grown bigger.

This is just a short summary of some of the atrocities I endured as a child. I have spared as much details as possible, because my intent is NOT to trigger, but to encourage you. In my case, I should have never had access to pornographic material within my home, even in the form of a cartoon. This shows the irresponsibility of my parental units for not enforcing safeguards to create a safe environment within the home. Secondly, there should have been healthy boundaries enforced between my father and I. I should've been disciplined and educated about the boundaries that were crossed when I first entered his master bedroom. My father could've educated me and said, "This is an area for adults and you are not allowed to come in here." Instead, he chose to steal his daughter's innocence, and like Tamar, I covered my head with shame for the majority of my childhood; this went on until adulthood.

The biggest issue that I find in childhood abuse victims is the need to justify and/or defend the actions of their abuser. I unfairly placed the blame on myself. I wore a blanket of shame. The reality of the matter is that I was the VICTIM. I DID NOT deserve the deep shame and disgrace that I felt to the core. The shame rightfully belonged to my abuser. Look at it this way. My abuser who committed the crime deserved to wear the badge of dishonor or the scarlet letter. I, the victim, needed space and time to heal. Unfortunately, as children, most of us don't have the luxury of running away from our abusers. We aren't provided with the resources or numbers to call in order to get the help we need. Therefore, we silently learn to grit our teeth and bury the pain inside.

Stockholm syndrome is a psychological coping mechanism that occurs when hostages or abuse victims bond with their captors or abusers. These victims eventually come to sympathize with their abusers and over time may begin to feel as if they share a similar vision (Reference: Healthline/ What is Stockholm Syndrome and Who Does it Affect?). Why do abused children internalize shame? It is simply a method used to survive. Our young minds are unable to cope with the truth that our own fathers and/or mothers could be evil and want to hurt us. If we choose to see our fathers and/or mothers as bad, it would force us to confront our own reality. Therefore, we could potentially lose our sanity. Young children need their parents to survive. Their parents provide for their basic necessities: food, water, and shelter. Just like plants need water, soil, and sunlight, children also need love and belonging. Self-preservation kicks in. She learns to excuse the behavior of her abuser so that she could see him as 'good.' Children cannot see the gray area. Children can often only see life through black and white lenses. It's either good or bad. Split thinking helps them make sense of their world. In order to accept the 'good' we see in our parents, such as when they would cook us meals or take care of us when we were ill, we in turn, place the blame on ourselves so we could *justify* their crimes. Children often think thoughts like, "If only I hadn't entered in the bathroom that day, then my father wouldn't have done weird things to me." Children also think, "I am bad. It is my fault. I did wrong. That is why Daddy is touching me." The truth is, the child is a victim of circumstances. The child has *no* choice in what kind of household she was brought up in, who her parents were, and what kind of neighborhood she grew up in. Truth is that her father is a sexually perverse adult. He is simply an adult man who cannot control his own loins. He has willingly decided to cross the boundaries of his young daughter in order to gratify his sexual lusts. That is HIS sin! It is not the daughter's fault.

One of the lies that I held close to my heart was, "I deserved the abuse because I was curious about sex." To dispel the first lie: "By age five, most children have asked some questions about sex, such as where babies come from, physical differences between males and females, body organs and functions, and the coming of another baby" (Reference: Washington Department/ Sexual Behavior and Children: When Is It a Problem and What to Do About It). My parents failed to appropriately educate me about sex. That was their crime, not mine. My curiosity DID NOT justify the cruelty and maltreatment that I endured.

Another lie that I believed was, "I caused my father to sexually abuse me because I desired to humiliate him by seeing him naked." The desire to humiliate my father was wrong, but the reality is my father's sin was even greater in the eyes of God.

> **Matthew 18:6:** But whoever causes one of these little ones who believe in me to sin, it would be better for him to have a great millstone fastened around his neck and to be drowned in the depth of the sea (ESV).

God despises people who hurt His children. It disgusts God. My sin to humiliate my father, at worst, should have been met with appropriate education of boundaries and some disciplinary action. It should have NEVER resulted in SEXUAL ABUSE. In fact, if there was a healthy family structure originally constructed, my desire to humiliate my father at the tender age of seven would have never run in my mind. Young girls, from healthy family structures revere, honor, and respect their fathers. It is only when the father does not act in his proper place that he destroys the foundation of order. Previously said, a house divided cannot stand. My father destroyed his house with his own hands.

Eventually, my father's 'business trips' were prolonged. The duration he was away from home became longer. I felt great joy when my father left; I was in eighth grade at that time. From then on, I wouldn't see my father again for another two years. My soul was at rest. Originally, I never planned on telling my mother about the sexual abuse that I endured by the hands of my father.

My mother and I had a very rocky relationship during my childhood. As I grew older, our relationship slowly but gradually improved. Although my mother wasn't nurturing, she played the best 'father' she could, and I excelled in academics and extracurricular activities. When I was a freshmen in high school, we lost our house to foreclosure. This was not sudden or surprising news. I was always preparing for the day that we would lose our home, because I knew of the debt collectors that called day-in and day-out. To be quite honest, it was a blessing in disguise. Our old house had become grimy and dirty. I was covered in fleabites whenever I slept. The new home was in a neighborhood nearby. It was a clean, one-story space.

One afternoon, I broke the news to my mother. I had planned to hold on to the secret until I was 18 and had left the house. The weight became too heavy to bear and I told her. She interrogated me several times, but she chose to believe me. To be honest, if my mother hadn't believed me, I might've lost my mind. Our Father in heaven knows how much we can bear. Unfortunately, many childhood sexual abuse survivors keep their stories to themselves. The first step to healing is to speak up. I encourage you to tell a safe, trusted friend or adult. May the Holy Spirit guide you to a safe person. Burdens are meant to be shared, not carried alone. Maya Angelou writes, "There is no greater agony than bearing an untold story inside you."

Chapter 3

An Introduction to Coping Mechanisms and Toxic Mindsets

Satan's agenda is to destroy the family system. "The job of parents is to model. Modeling includes how to be a man or woman; how to relate intimately to another person; how to acknowledge and express emotions; how to fight fairly; how to have physical, emotional and intellectual boundaries; how to communicate; how to cope and survive life's unending problems; how to be self-disciplined; and how to love oneself and another. Shame-based parents cannot do any of these. They simply don't know how" (Reference: Healing the Shame that Binds You, John Bradshaw). Our first introduction of the triune God is demonstrated through our parental units. The role of the father is to protect, support, and give identity to the child. The role of the mother is to comfort and teach children. Grievously, many trauma survivors have not grown up in families where protection, support, identity, comfort, and instruction were demonstrated to us. As I mentioned above, a plant needs water, sunlight, and soil to survive. When the plant lacks water, for example, its roots can potentially stretch beyond its original extent in order to attempt to reach the closest body of water. This is what happens to children who grow up in toxic environments. We become like the malnourished plant, and are stretched and forced to prematurely grow outside of our comfort zones. When we are prematurely stretched outside of our comfort zones, we develop coping mechanisms; these are unhealthy but necessary methods to aid in our survival. As adults, these coping mechanisms prove to be unhelpful. These cognitive distortions listed below demonstrate a skewed perception of reality. This distorted reality is NOT based on truth, but based on emotions, thoughts, or negative self-talk.

Polarized thinking: This is the most common mindset found in trauma survivors. It is also known as black-and-white thinking or all-or-nothing thinking. In my life, I have to often wrestle down this coping mechanism. For example, let's say you instant messaged your best friend and she normally replies within a short time span. This time, you haven't heard from her in a week. You might think, "Either she messages me tomorrow, or she might as well not be my friend anymore." A more healthy and gray area mindset would look at the situation objectively without tying our childhood feelings into the present day circumstance. Most likely, I am projecting something that occurred in my past onto my friend in the present moment. Does this kind of situation call for the response of this magnitude? Has my friend generally been consistent? What happened to me in my childhood? A healthier way of thinking might be, "My friend is usually consistent and messages me on time. She might have her own personal issues at this moment and cannot meet my need. I can try to find another way to meet my emotional need without her. Yes I'm disappointed in her, but one small failure doesn't equate to termination of friendship." When we think in opposite extremes, this presents a good opportunity for us to trace back our emotions to a specific event that occurred when we were small. This

An Introduction to Coping Mechanisms and Toxic Mindsets

is a good opportunity to grieve and connect to the little girl that was hurt a long time ago.

Disqualifying the positive: There might be something positive happening at the moment. Due to fear of loss, uncertainty, or anger, we are afraid of looking at the positive aspects involved. We are terrified of the potential of the negative happening. An example of this might occur when a friend tells you that you are beautiful. You might automatically draw the conclusion that they are just saying a nice fact about you because of your relational connection, not because they really see that in you. In my personal life, a trigger of mine is when the opposite gender comments positively on my appearance. In my mind, I associate a man calling me beautiful as, "I just want to sleep with you. You are nothing more to me than a sex object." Clearly this demonstrates a triggering point to me. I associate a man's positive compliment towards my physical appearance as his hidden motive to potentially sexually abuse me. I have to intentionally wrestle down this trigger point and choose to believe the person has a positive intent, especially if the person proves to be genuinely harmless. A more healthy way of thinking would be, "This brother in Christ simply commented on my physical appearance just to be kind. He doesn't want to date, pursue, or rape me. He's just being nice. Just because he finds me physically attractive doesn't mean he is going to force himself upon me. I find clouds beautiful. I find trees beautiful. I don't want to have sex with clouds or trees. I might not even be his type." The text listed above is quite long. Often, when I wrestle a thought down, I have to preach a miniature sermon to myself, so I will not dwell on the lies.

Magnification/ Minimization:
An example of magnification would be catastrophizing. Simply put, catastrophizing is expecting the absolute worse outcome to a particular situation. For example, when I was in undergrad, every time I thought about my future, I imagined myself to be homeless on the streets with a cup in my hand, begging for change. The trigger point was whenever I spent a little more than my carefully controlled budget. I worried that I would misspend my way into poverty, similar to what my father did. My line of thinking would be, "I overspent this

month. I'm going to end up homeless." A healthier line of thinking would be, "Well, this isn't ideal. I hoped to be able to meet my budget this month, but I didn't. I might have to eat out less this month, but I will be okay."

Rumination: The best way to describe rumination is to imagine a track in your brain. On the track, there are various sentences. The sentence that runs the fastest compared to the other sentences in the marathon of your mind is the one that wins your attention. Nine out of ten times, rumination is centered in on a negative thought. Rumination on a positive thought often is found in maladaptive daydreaming. A young woman constantly entrenched with the ideas of marrying is ruminating on her fantasy of marriage in order to escape her reality. Fear of man allows us to spend too much time ruminating on what others perceive of us. "My pastor hates me. He really hates me. I must have offended him!" These are thoughts that I have to constantly cast down. This happens when I begin to worship man instead of God, and I need to repent for allowing fear of man to become a snare. To stop ruminating, I often plead the

An Introduction to Coping Mechanisms and Toxic Mindsets

blood of Christ over my mind, and I intentionally choose to focus my mind on how much God adores me.

Emotional Reasoning: Emotional reasoning is allowing your feelings to become the reality of a situation. *I feel stripped away from all my dignity, therefore I am a worthless person. I feel ugly, therefore I am ugly. I feel stupid, therefore I must be stupid.* The examples listed above are lies that I believed due to trusting in my feelings more than truth. Feelings often act as indicators for us to understand the symptoms. We trace these feelings in order to get to the root of these symptoms. Once we understand the root, we can counteract the root with the truth. In cognitive behavioral therapy (CBT), a therapist interrogates your line of reasoning, thereby, feelings and actions change. Thoughts◊Feelings◊Behaviors are said to be a train reaction. Whereby, in order to counteract a negative thought, we often begin with what we are feeling. To illustrate, we might currently feel an overwhelming sense of anxiety. The anxiety shows up in a nervous stomach or intense headaches. The root of the issue stems from our thinking. You might ask yourself, "What am I thinking?" Your thoughts might swarm with fear of losing your home and fear of not being able to pay your rent on time. Those are legitimate fears, but constantly ruminating on the fear will not solve the matter at hand. The feeling of anxiety ceases when you form a plan and set a deadline. In my personal life, sometimes life gets extremely busy and I have many assignments to complete. In order for me to have peace of mind, I often write down my feelings, the cognitive distortion that I believe, and a truth to counteract the distortion. I might feel like I'm going to die due to the amount of work I need to accomplish. I recognize that I'm emotionally reasoning. The truth of the matter is that I have a lot to do, but I can and will finish my tasks. I must create a schedule and prioritize assignments based on deadlines. My feeling of anxiety minimizes when I form a concrete action plan.

Control Fallacy: There are two kinds of control fallacies: external and internal locus of control. With internal locus of control, I feel responsible for other people's behaviors, attitudes, feelings, thoughts, and choices.

An Introduction to Coping Mechanisms and Toxic Mindsets

Trauma survivors often have trouble separating their own feelings from someone else's feelings. A good example of this is demonstrated in a game of tennis. Let's say that you miss the ball, and you do not hit it past the net. If your teammate yells and curses, you should not feel responsible for that person's anger. Yes, he is angry for losing the championship, but that is *his* anger, not *your* anger. Your teammate is responsible for dealing with his own feelings, and he should not emotionally manipulate you, so that you would feel guilt and shame for missing the ball. You can emphasize with his loss, but you must remember that you and your teammate are separate individuals with separate feelings.

Another toxic mindset a trauma survivor has is an external locus of control. This is often called victim mentality or learned helplessness. The following story that I share below is to help dispel the fact that you are merely just a victim.

> **Romans 8:37:** No, in all these things we are more than conquerors through him who loved us (ESV).

An Introduction to Coping Mechanisms and Toxic Mindsets

    The victim mentality is the mindset that I had to wrestle down and I hope that you would be able to see yourself as a person who has the potential to hurt others too. Otherwise, it's easy to stay stuck in a perpetual toxic cycle of blame and refuse to move forward in your life. With every prey, there is a predator. With every predator, there is a prey. In the food chain, everyone is a victim and everyone is a perpetrator. When we remain victims, vicious predators will constantly chase us. It is only when we take *healthy* responsibility for the crimes we committed that we can move forward in life and find freedom.

    In elementary school, there was a girl named Annette who'd recently moved to the States from a Southeast Asian country. She and I were both Chinese. This common background united us at first, but I was a terrible friend. Our mothers even became friends at one point. When the popular, wealthy girls whom I desperately wanted to fit in with made fun of her, I chose not to stand up for her. In the end, I ignored her, and at times, I participated in making fun of her by laughing amongst the crowd. This was very wrong of me and I had to repent of my sin to God. Annette, an unbeliever, chose to forgive me years later when I apologized to her. I didn't deserve her kindness. That's why we should be merciful because others have been merciful to us. Just as my biological father betrayed my very trust, I betrayed Annette's trust in me by not sticking up for her. Most of all, Jesus Christ was merciful to me when I was just one of the many sinners who stripped Him of His dignity and nailed Him to the cross. If I want to receive God's forgiveness for my sins committed against humanity, I must be willing to forgive others, even when it hurts (Matthew 6:14-15). Forgiveness is NOT pardoning or excusing the criminal's action. It's NOT denying the pain they have inflicted and the many years of psychological damage that will follow after. It's choosing to walk in freedom by allowing God's justice to happen His way and in His time. Forgiveness is the gift I give to myself, so I will no longer drink the bitter poison of hate. In my life, forgiveness was a choice I had to make every single day until all the hate in my heart went away. Do not be hard on yourself if forgiveness is a daily surrendering of anger, hate, and bitterness. True forgiveness comes

An Introduction to Coping Mechanisms and Toxic Mindsets

after much grief.

Fallacy of change: This is a false belief that a human being can hold the power to change others. On the contrary, God is the only one who can change our hearts. Trauma survivors often hold on to an abusive boyfriend or unhealthy situationship because they are accustomed to breadcrumbs of kindness. Like a dog that is used to eating leftover bones from their owners, we are so starved for affection that leftovers look like five-star meals. Looking back in my life, I was hungry for male affection. When I was in the sixth grade, I was a notorious crybaby. It seemed that my tear ducts failed to escape me. I had a friend named Logan who would help me open up my locker and help me with my math homework. Logan also seemed to have an endless supply of tissues ready for me whenever I cried in class. My 12-year old self ended up developing the biggest crush on Logan, and when we reunited in high school, he'd changed for the worse. I was unwilling to let him go, because I clung to the image of the 12-year-old superman who came and dove to my rescue. I clung to him despite the fact that our

An Introduction to Coping Mechanisms and Toxic Mindsets

relationship was pretty toxic. In my heart, I was hoping he would change for the better, but he never did. We called each other names, and we pulled each other's hair. This went on for some time until one day, I had enough. My friendship with him ended. Maya Angelou says, "When someone shows you who they are, believe them the first time."

Chapter 4

The Obsession for Romantic Love & Satanic Agenda of a Fatherless Generation

Due to coping mechanisms, you learned to ignore the red flags in your previous relationships. Just as you would've stayed for an ex who beat you, called you names, slept with multiple women, be sure to stay for your pastor or the leaders who've made minor mistakes. Learn to ignore those 'red flags' or imperfections in your leaders and peers. The red flags you see in your leaders are a fraction of what you experienced as a child. Their actions trigger past memories, and these memories bring out the present fear in you. It's not fair to be more judgmental of people whose sins and imperfections trigger your past pain. In psychology, this is a defense mechanism called projection. You project your unresolved pain onto others. Hurt people hurt people. Excuse your offenders. Excuse your peers. Of course, be wise. Be discerning. It is your responsibility to learn how to discern the spirits. Learn to not be petty, and learn to be generous with forgiveness. Every time you are offended, circle it back to yourself. Confront the log in your eye. Many times, God uses a person we don't like in order to help us grow in the fruits of the Holy Spirit. Ask God, "What kind of fruit do you want me to grow through this person?" If you can't wrestle the offense down through prayer, confront the person. An example of being unable to wrestle down offense is when everything that the offender does feels offensive. This offense is like a brick wall that prevents you from receiving from that person. Schedule an individual meeting with the offender. Let them know what they did wrong, and how you perceived it on your end. Many times, it's just a misunderstanding or communication issue. Surround yourself with people who are mature in their walk with the Lord and can see your leaders in a balanced light. Whenever you have an issue and are tempted to leave, you can talk to those mature people. They will give you a fresh perspective to your offense. An example of this in my life is that I had a distorted view of my apostle. This occurred due to my own immaturity. As a babe in Christ, I had yet to develop my own discernment, and I just listened to what another sister told me about him. Satan planted a lie in my life that he was planting a cult and he didn't care about people. Satan kept telling me that the apostle hated me. He wanted to use the congregation's spiritual gifts to spread his own personal agenda. He just cared about numbers, and the amount of people that came to know the Lord. I told a mature sister who was committed to the church. She was able to give me a completely different perspective based on her experience with the apostle. As time went on, I was able to see that he cared about the issues that went on in my life and not just the fact that I was spiritually gifted in evangelism. Satan wants to destroy covenant relationships. If God reveals a leaders' imperfection, you are supposed to cover the leader in prayer. You are the watchman of the church.

When you first enter in a church that is specialty focused (i.e. deliverance, evangelism, prophecy), don't be so quick to present your gift. It is best to hide your gift. You need to grow in the basics of faith. In your own immaturity, you will feel used and become bitter as you serve in your gift. Due to your immaturity, you will find your identity and value in your gift, so you don't know how to say no. When you burnout because of your gift, you will be quick to point fingers and blame your leaders for manipulating you. It is you who made the mistake and was too eager to present your gift to the church. Yes, you are gifted. You are a gifted baby. You need to grow in character and serve the people that God has placed above you. Honor your leaders, and honor will be bestowed upon you. If you first enter in a church focused on outreach and evangelism, a wise leader will not send you to the Middle East upon your first interest in missions. They might not even teach you how to street evangelize. Perhaps, they'll give you an assignment that seems beneath you. You want to cry out, "Don't you see, I'm so gifted!" Yes, you are gifted. Usually, the more gifted you are, the more mentally ill and unstable you are, the more deliverance and counseling you also need. Hurt people hurt people.

The Obsession for Romantic Love & Satanic Agenda of a Fatherless Generation

I was the exception to this case. When I first came to East Asia, I met a local missionary. She was on staff for two years of missions. I was heartbroken at the time and confided in her about the *man I loved*. I also excitedly confided in her that I loved sharing the gospel. This was because I had shared the gospel on my campus back in Texas. In my case, I skipped much protocol that most people have to endure to go on long-term missions. I also suffered much warfare because of that. I had demonic dreams. I also had insomnia for two to three months. I also had rebellion and rejection issues, so I was double-minded. My lust manifested when I met seekers to do Bible studies in coffee shops. Instead of being quiet to hide my identity, I talked loudly to try to get the attention of the cute boy sitting across the room.

Order is there for a reason. You might argue that if I was able to skip order, why can't you? Just because a man drives one hundred miles per hour, hits a tree, and doesn't die, should everyone else do the same? I don't recommend jumping into the mission field without consistently serving in your home country. God had a specific plan for my life at that specific time. I was the exception. If you can't be faithful and consistent at home, how can you be faithful outside of your home? If you don't earn the trust of your leaders, why do you deserve to jump on a platform? God needs to take you through a process where selfish ambition, pride, and envy are stripped out of you before you enter the mission field.

      I illustrate the point above so I can help paint a romantic picture. Just like order is required to become a missionary, order is required to become a wife. You don't wake up one fine morning and simply become a wife. God takes you through a process so that you will be prepared to meet your God-ordained husband. During this process, your pride, envy, selfishness, rejection, abandonment, contentiousness, rebellion, and insecurities are stripped out of you. Let's say you are a woman who has unresolved issues from her past. You meet a man before God refines and heals you. Broken you will attract broken him. The first several years of your marriage will be hell. Your insecurity will breed clinginess. This will irk and suffocate the man. Your brokenness will lead you to marry a man who is addicted, prideful, lustful, bound, entitled, and/or physically abusive. If you don't die outside of marriage, you will die inside of marriage. If you marry when you are whole and healed, you might have a marriage without any arguments. Because you died outside of marriage, you can focus on loving one another and building God's Kingdom together.

As mentioned earlier, crippling coping mechanisms are formed during our upbringing where we were not modeled healthy relationships and boundaries. This brings a lot of confusion and dysfunction when we begin to enter the realm of courtship. Often, the assumption is made that we can simply dive headfirst into romantic love. Premature romantic love creates confusion, brokenness, and deepened hurt. If you were a child from a broken family system, romantic love is not the solution to your deep mother and father wounds. Those wounds can only be healed by our heavenly Father. He will send us the right people and resources to aid us in our healing journey. When we attempt to entertain romantic imaginations, situations, or actual relationships before we develop into who we are, we only end up delaying our healing process. A practical example is illustrated in animal breeding.

> "Even though your dog may actually have 2 reproductive cycles in a year, your female dog is mono-estrous. Meaning? Your dog only has one breeding season every year. And when do dogs first go into heat? Their heat cycle may begin as early as 6 months to 1 year and at this age onward, mating and pregnancy can occur.
> If your female dog becomes a mama dog as early as her first heat, she may not know how to act in this motherhood situation and may not fully grasp the responsibility of being a mother, leading to not taking good care of or rejecting her pups" (Pet Parents Brand, Why Breeding Your Dog on Her First Heat is Not OK).

As a responsible dog owner will heavily protect her female puppies during her first heat, God aggressively protects His daughters from perverted male society. Many of the men we have dictated to be *the one* were simply Satan in handsome flesh. Some of those one-sided unrequited relationships left me crying for years after the men were gone. Now, I see this as God's protection to prevent me from completely losing myself. These men later proved to be distractions sent by the enemy who deterred me from my journey to wholeness. In my life, I had many quick encounters with men that caused me to paint a fantasy in my mind; this was because of my childhood voids. A void is a dark place without wisdom, knowledge, and revelation. What I had defined as love at the time was actually lust and obsession. The feelings of euphoria that accompanied me when a new object of my affection appeared in my life stirred the longing inside of me to be held and loved. Due to the fact that I was sexualized at a young age, my automatic association with love was butterflies in my stomach and sweaty palms. Now, I see butterflies as red flags. These butterflies are my internal system alerting me to danger. In my particular case, my parental units' inconsistent attachment led me to fear intimacy and closeness. This actually proved to be a helpful defense mechanism that kept my numerous one-sided soul ties from becoming physical. Every time I reached a level of emotional intimacy with a clown in a crown that I felt uncomfortable with, I put on my running shoes and ran. This proved to be effective until I was a freshman in high school and I met a man who was six years my senior. I thought he was *different* than the others. In reality, he touched a part of my brokenness that no other boy my age had been able to reach. He touched the rawness of the wound that my father left. It took me five complete years to finally let him go. If I had entered any of those relationships prematurely, I would've become even more lost than I already was. When a female puppy is prematurely pregnant, she has not fully mentally and physically developed to understand her role and place in her puppies' lives. God has given us roles and places in His Kingdom that He wants us to fulfill before we meet our mates. He wants us to speak to our wounds, clean the shards of glass left in the cuts, stitch up the bleeding flesh until we are fully restored and recognize our inherent value. He wants us to intimately know Him as a Father, friend, and husband. He wants to be all things to us, and then, He will give us a revelation of our calling. He will also open our eyes to who we really are. We can't walk in our complete God given authority that He places within us if we are entertaining a clown with a crown. Is there a man in your life that God wants you to drop like a bag of hot bricks?

The Bible instructs young women, "O daughters of Jerusalem, I adjure you: Do not arouse or awaken love until the time is right" (Songs of Solomon 8:4, Berean Study Bible). God is the only one who can really determine when the time is right and when the gift of romantic love will benefit and not harm us.

This is equivalent to presenting a car to a two-year-old girl. A two-year-old in her diapers is not going to appreciate or enjoy the gift. Giving her a new BMW and a set of car keys will only bring a confused look upon her face. This gift is actually a burden and not a blessing. When the young girl reaches the tender age of 16, she is ready to receive the BMW and her shiny set of car keys. A responsible parent will keep the gift in hiding until she is mature enough to receive the blessing.

The obsession of romantic love is a symptom of a fatherless generation. Our Father in heaven is a God of rules, order, structure, authority, and protocol. There are systems that He has enacted out for human beings to ensure our well-being on this Earth.

> **Genesis 1:28:** God blessed them and said to them, "Be fruitful and increase in number; fill the earth and subdue it. Rule over the fish in the sea and the birds in the sky and over every living creature that moves on the ground." <u>God gave Adam authority to dominate the animals. The animals were subject to Adam's position</u> (NIV).

> **Romans 5:13-14:** For sin indeed was in the world before the law was given, but sin is not counted where there is no law. Yet death reigned from Adam to Moses, even over those whose sinning was not like the **transgression of Adam**, who

was a type of the one who was to come (ESV).

Genesis 3:12: The man said, "The woman whom you gave to be with me, she gave me fruit of the tree, and I ate" (ESV).

Noted above, Adam tries to assign the blame to Eve, but the reality of the matter is the greater responsibility falls on Adam because he is her covering. God specifically commands Adam to not eat from the Tree of the Knowledge of Good and Evil (Genesis 2:16-17). Adam is Eve's spiritual covering and He is responsible for her since she came from his side. Arguably speaking, Eve was deceived. Yet, perhaps Adam did not give her clear instructions because Eve misunderstood God's command. Eve perceived it as such, "But God said, 'You shall not eat of the fruit of the tree that is in the midst of the garden, **neither shall you touch it**, lest you die" (Genesis 3:3, (ESV). In the New Testament, teachers will be judged with greater strictness during the day of Judgment (James 3:1, ESV). Teachers are held with greater accountability for their sins because they are leaders. People look to them for instruction and direction. Yes, it is the individual student's responsibility to test the spirits and discern if what the teacher is saying aligns with God's Word. God judges people in positions of authority more harshly.

The purpose of the text above is to illustrate how the father and/or husband is in a position of authority. His sphere of influence is his children and wife. Just like Adam was held accountable for Eve's deception, the father and/or husband is held responsible for the structure of his family. He is the leader and the head of the home, just like Jesus is the head of the body, the church. When the man in the family fails to play the role of a responsible leader, God holds him accountable. When the man of the home abuses his position of authority, this creates a negative domino effect that impacts the mother and children; this is why God judges those who misuse their authority harshly.

Satan came into my home at a young age to destroy my ability to submit to authority. Due to several terrible experiences at home,

God had to demonstrate numerous corrective experiences in order for me to trust in the fact that not *all* authority figures have bad intentions and motives. Remember, the cognitive distortions mentioned above. Just because you had one tormenting abusive experience with authority, this does not mean that all authority is Satan in disguise. We need to learn to think in a balanced manner and to discern the spirits for ourselves.

> **Matthew 7:15-20:** Beware of false prophets, who come to you in sheep's clothing, but inwardly they are ravenous wolves. <u>You will know them by their fruits</u>. Do men gather grapes from thornbushes or figs from thistles? Even so, every good tree bears good fruit, but a bad tree bears bad fruit. A good tree cannot bear bad fruit, nor *can* a bad tree bear good fruit. Every tree that does not bear good fruit is cut down and thrown into the fire. Therefore by their fruits you will know them (NKJV).

The Obsession for Romantic Love & Satanic Agenda of a Fatherless Generation

The reason why Satan wants to destroy family systems is because he wants to destroy marriage. Healthy marriage is God's way of putting His fingerprints on this world. This is equivalent to indiscreetly spreading the gospel to all nations. It's God's strategy for showing lost people that genuine love exists. Satan hates love because when he was thrown out of heaven, he knew that he would never experience love again (Revelation 12:7-9). Satan wants to destroy marriage so that the next generation will be unable to experience *true* love and genuinely love others. God is love. Satan is hate. The only true polarized statement that we need to remember is how God is light and Satan is darkness. When children are traumatized in their family of origin, nine out of ten times, they will severely hate or mistrust God. In my life, a dear friend of mine told me about God in seventh grade, but I hated Him because I falsely blamed Him for all the pain that had been inflicted on me by my parents. I was a tortured soul and the question I asked God in my prayers was, "If you love me, why did my dad sexually abuse me?" I would even say, "I hate you, God." I would curse in my prayers and I would curse at God.

God, in His rich love and mercy, had compassion on me. When I was a senior in high school, I prayed to God, although I didn't believe in Him at the time. I told God that if He would never let me be financially poor again, I would follow Him for the rest of my life. Like Jacob, I wrestled with God in prayer until God gave me His blessing. The blessing was several scholarships so I could go to a highly ranked university in my state without any debt to my name. Otherwise, I would have gone to the local college in my town.

> **Genesis 32:22-32:** That night Jacob got up and took his two wives, his two female servants and his eleven sons and crossed the ford of the Jabbok. After he had sent them across the stream, he sent over all his possessions. So Jacob was left alone, and a man wrestled with him till daybreak. **When the man saw that he could not overpower him, he touched the socket of Jacob's hip so that his hip was wrenched as he wrestled with the man.** Then the man said, "Let me go, for it is daybreak."

But Jacob replied, "I will not let you go unless you bless me."
The man asked him, "What is your name?"
"Jacob," he answered.
Then the man said, "Your name will no longer be Jacob, but Israel, because you have struggled with God and with humans and have overcome."
Jacob said, "Please tell me your name." But he replied, "Why do you ask my name?" **Then he blessed him there.**
So Jacob called the place Peniel, saying, "It is because I saw God face to face, and yet my life was spared."
The sun rose above him as he passed Peniel, and he was limping because of his hip. Therefore to this day the Israelites do not eat the tendon attached to the socket of the hip, because the socket of Jacob's hip was touched near the tendon.

Little did I know at the time, as I was wrestling God in prayer for blessing, I was also praying the prayer of Jabez. I do admit that I was not honoring God at the time with my lifestyle, but God is compassionate and gives us gifts we don't deserve (NIV).

1 Chronicles 4:9-10: Now Jabez was more honorable than his brothers. His mother had named him Jabez, saying, "Because I bore him **in pain**."
And Jabez called out to the God of Israel, "**If only You would bless me and enlarge my territory! May Your hand be with me and keep me from harm, so that I will be free from pain.**" And God granted the request of Jabez (Berean Bible Study).

Jabez was an honorable man who was cursed with pain since his birth. We do not know the exact reason why he was born in pain, yet God saw him as honorable. I don't know why or how God saw me as honorable, but He did. He heard my cry and pitied my every groan. I beseech you, even if you don't believe in God yet, cry out to Him with your honest, unfiltered speech, because God hears our cries. Like He heard my cry, He will hear yours too.

Due to the lack of healthy love demonstrated in my family of origin, I wrestled to believe that God is a good and caring Father. This is why I had to wrestle like Jacob and pray the prayer of Jabez.

Sin is perversion of God's original design. This chain reaction illustrates God's dominion and the level of dominion He assigns to each of His creations.

God→Men→Animals
God→Men→Women→Animals
God→Men→Women→Children

God gave men a measure of authority over women. God gave men and women a measure of authority over the animals in the Earth. God gave women and men a measure of authority over their children.

> **Genesis 1:26:** And God said, Let us make man in our image, after our likeness: and let them have **dominion** over the fish of the sea, and over the fowl of the air, and over the cattle, and

over all the earth, and over every creeping thing that creepeth upon the earth (KJV).

Genesis 1:28: And God blessed them, and God said unto them, Be fruitful, and multiply, and replenish the earth, and subdue it: and have **dominion** over the fish of the sea, and over the fowl of the air, and over every living thing that moveth upon the earth (KJV).

The NASB Hebrew concordance states that dominion is Hebrew for *radah.* Dominion is also a synonymous to subjugation. To subjugate simply means that God gave men a level of control over women. Oxford Languages define control as "the power to influence or direct people's behavior or the course of events." Simply put, God gave men a level of influence over the women who are placed in their lives. The men in women's lives either influence them positively or negatively. They can impart strength into a woman or they strip away a woman's dignity. It is up to the men of this generation to choose if they want to be strength givers or strength takers, depending on how they interact, view, and treat their fellow women. The word control tends to bring terror for a trauma survivor. This is because we have experienced authority figures who abused their power. We were stripped away of our dignity, and we were never given a choice over the atrocities that were committed against us. A healthy, confident, secure strength giver will never shove his influence down a woman's throat and force her to chew it up. He, instead, will live his life in an imperfect, yet, exemplary fashion, which invokes the woman to admire his influence and, in turn, she will naturally follow his lead.

In this day and age, most women were raised by fathers who were strength takers or absent fathers. Instead of imparting knowledge, wisdom, and revelation into their daughters, they neglected their God given roles. I always wondered why some nonbeliever marriages were prosperous and successful. This is because they unknowingly followed Kingdom principals, which garnered the favor of God on their marriages and families. Unfortunately, when Satan deceived Eve, sin entered in the world. Satan's intent was to destroy God's order. The reality is that the majority of families in America do not follow God's principals. Forty to fifty percent of American marriages end in divorce (Reference: American Psychological Association, Marriage & Divorce).

In turn, the order of this world has become the chain reaction displayed below.

Satan→Women→Men→God

In many family systems, due to the lack of respect for the poor quality of men that they chose to be married to, the women usurp the authority God places on their husbands. These women unknowingly invite the Jezebel spirit into their lives. Jezebel was a Phoenician princess who came from the land of idols. She marries King Ahab of Israel. She usurps Ahab's authority and uses his position to fulfill her agenda of killing off God's prophets. Ahab is a self-pitying, weak-willed, insecure man who abdicates his authority to Jezebel. When one does something out of God's order, they invite the demonic realm into their lives. For this reason, those who rebel against God given authority experience much spiritual warfare.

Genesis 3:15 (NIV) depicts the curse between Satan and the woman.

> *"And I will put enmity between you and the woman, and between your offspring and hers; he will crush your head, and you will strike his heel."*

When Satan deceived Eve, the curse entered in the world. The curse of sin is passed down from one generation to the very next. Essentially, the woman's children walk around with a bruised heel. Some of us have come from long lines of women who never overcame their personal traumas. Therefore, they married the very men sent by the enemy to destroy their God given purpose. The generation of bruised women continued to come down from your ancestry line until the day you came out of the womb. Satan messed with the wrong daughter when he picked you. You will be the daughter who will crush the serpent's head. You will destroy the works of the enemy! The generational curses that Satan has spoke over your family since the beginning of time will cease to exist. You are the generation that will begin the blessings for future generations to come. Satan, get behind thee!

Chapter 5

Broken Perception, Insecurity, and the World's Scale

What is love? Is it butterflies in your stomach? Is it when a man gazes into your pupils and tells you that you are the most beautiful woman he has ever laid his eyes on? Is it when an attractive man moves you to tears by his acts of kindness? Is it being so afraid to approach a person whose flesh mesmerizes you? Is it when an attractive man spends money on you? Is it spending all day and night fantasizing about your object of affection and dreaming about the future plans that you two may have together?

I would like to challenge you and say that what you are defining as love is actually the result of unprocessed voids. There is a deep hole in your soul that is similar to a famished animal that uncontrollably devours anything that resembles food, even garbage from the dumpster. This is exactly what occurs when a young, single woman hasn't emerged from her chrysalis and still believes that she is but only a small caterpillar. In reality, she is actually a gorgeous, stunning butterfly. She internalizes all her trauma. The trauma acts as a barrier that distorts her view of herself. She cannot see herself as God sees her. Thus, she cannot recognize and distinguish the difference between a meal from a five-star restaurant and trash from the local dumpster.

The sad reality is that many trauma victims see themselves through a broken lens and crooked smile. Many of these young women cannot see their true value. The spirit of rejection entered into their lives at a young age, and rebellion followed thereafter. The spirit of rejection and rebellion created a baby together called double-mindedness. The young woman who bears these twins is unstable in all her ways and has adopted many false personalities in order to be accepted by her peers. The truth is that her real personality is what makes her unique, special, and powerful. Under her **auth**entic or true self, this is where her **auth**ority lies. Imagine this. Imagine that you are a red piece of round clay. The other pieces of clay are purple squares. In order for you to fit in the purple squares, you have to cut your round edges to create pointy ones, and then, mix yourself with blue clay so that you can become purple. You're essentially destroying yourself to fit into the constraints of other peoples' limited understanding. You lose your **auth**ority as you give up your **auth**enticity. In order to begin healing, she must seek therapy, get deliverance, and learn to walk in her authority. She must accept herself for who God created her to be, personality quirks and all. Unfortunately, due to this young women's bloodline, she has to go through many deliverances. Rejection is a strongman that opens the door for many other demons to enter into her life. When the demons are gone, she can finally have a clear mind to be able to unlearn the many lies that she has believed.

It is sin to see yourself less than how God sees you. The Word of God defines this mindset as having a grasshopper mentality. The Israelite community, upon encountering the Nephilim, the offspring of fallen angels and women, were intimidated. They looked at themselves as grasshoppers and compared themselves with others. The Israelites failed to recognize the power that they possessed. After all, God was on their side.

> **Numbers 13:26–33 (NIV):** They came back to Moses and Aaron and the whole Israelite community at Kadesh in the Desert of Paran. There they reported to them and to the whole assembly and showed them the fruit of the land. They gave Moses this account: "We went into the land to which you sent us, and it does flow with milk and honey! Here is its fruit. But the people who live there are powerful, and the cities are fortified and very large. We even saw descendants of Anak there. The Amalekites live in the Negev; the Hittites, Jebusites and Amorites live in the hill country; and the Canaanites live near the sea and along the Jordan."
> Then Caleb silenced the people before Moses and said, "We should go up and take possession of the land, for we can certainly do it."
> But the men who had gone up with him said, "<u>We can't attack those people; they are stronger than we are.</u>" And they

spread among the Israelites a bad report about the land they had explored. They said, "The land we explored devours those living in it. <u>All the people we saw there are of great size. We saw the Nephilim there (the descendants of Anak come from the Nephilim). We seemed like grasshoppers in our own eyes, and we looked the same to them</u>."

Young women who have been rejected struggle with insecurity. Insecurity is the gateway to jealousy. Jealousy opens up the door to envy. Envy opens up the door to sabotage. In my life, I was a very jealous and insecure woman. My father opened this door of comparison up when he was critical of my physical appearance. Sexual abuse from my father coupled with my mother's lack of nurture made me feel unloved. Growing up in financial difficulty made me feel even more rejected. I felt undesired by boys, and this was the straw that broke the camel's back. When I was in middle school, there was a girl with an incredibly cute laugh and she had pretty blue eyes. All the boys wanted her and I wanted to be like her. I was determined to mimic her personality from that day forward;

consequently, parts of my soul begin to chip off. As a young girl, I didn't know who I was, so I blended into my environments and my friends became my compasses. Every time I liked a boy, my personality would change to suit what I believed his preferences were. I began to develop false or demonic personalities as I picked up personalities from people I admired. When the deliverance minister cast out demons, she also cast out the false personalities. Now, I have my real personality back. It isn't the loud seductress who lures boys in with her damsel in distress tendencies. It's an introvert who likes to make soaps and write books. If a man cannot accept my real personality, he doesn't deserve me. Here is a snippet from my deliverance testimony as I was getting demons cast out of me:

> My mouth and face felt convoluted and I was manifesting by saying things like "Oh wee, wah, whyyy!" At moments, I felt like there was an evil-sounding man's voice coming out of my mouth.

Deliverance is just one of the avenues that God used on my journey towards completeness and wholeness. My story to healing from my three-year soul tie is a unique one, and your journey will be too. I have refrained from explaining demonology in detail, because I am new in this realm of knowledge. I still have a lot to learn in this area, and I hope to be able to cast demons out of people one day. If you are interested in this topic, I recommend a book called "Pigs in the Parlor: A Practical Guide to Deliverance" by Frank Hammond and Ida M. Hammond.

The Bible defines love as:

> **1 Corinthians 13:4-8:** Love is patient, love is kind. It does not envy, it does not boast, it is not proud. It does not dishonor others, it is not self-seeking, it is not easily angered, it keeps no record of wrongs. Love does not delight in evil but rejoices with the truth. It always protects, always trusts, always hopes, always perseveres. Love never fails. But where there are prophecies, they will cease; where there are tongues, they will be stilled; where there is knowledge, it will pass away (NIV).

Broken Perception, Insecurity, and the World's Scale

There are four kinds of love; they are: Storge, Philia, Eros, and Agape. In a healthy home, agape should be the foundation of love. Agape is divine love. It is the love of God. If agape is the foundation, the two parents are interdependent to one another and do not display an unhealthy level of co-dependency. Storge is family love. It's the love of a mother to her child. The sad reality is that many trauma victims start out life crippled, because they were never demonstrated healthy storge love. Philia is the love you would have for your friend. If a child grows up in a healthy storge, she knows how to philia someone. Many trauma survivors rush into eros as an attempt to shortstop the pain. In fact, they are only delaying their processes of healing. The broken little girl who was sexually abused at the tender age of seven cannot be healed through eros. Eros is romantic love. This kind of love is reserved for mature adults. Arrested development is being stuck at the age when the trauma occurred. Inside the trauma survivor, there lies a little girl. God has to grow this little girl up to her real age in the natural. God does this through people. He places trauma survivors in spiritual families where they are demonstrated healthy storge. Sadly,

Broken Perception, Insecurity, and the World's Scale

many trauma survivors sabotage these relationships because of their own dysfunction.

    The summer I graduated from undergrad, I enrolled myself in counseling. This was the last straw. I saw an unhealthy pattern in my life. I was tired of running away. The first session at the counselor's office, I felt uncomfortable and nervous. This was a complete stranger, and I had to confide in her what had occurred. She immediately traced my obsession with boys back to the root. The fatherless wound was real. By God's grace, she was a kind Christian woman, and I was able to disclose my honest thoughts to her. Every week she gave me a chapter of a book to read and a writing assignment. This went on for several weeks until I left for East Asia. The book was called Not Marked by Mary Demuth. In it she writes:

> The yard of your life has been invaded by pests, weed seeds, invasive plants, and all sorts of riffraff. The sexual abuse you've experienced has set you back, has marred your spot on this earth. It's not fair. It stinks. And it makes life seem impossible to you. But it happened, and

here you are surrounded by a jungle of pain.

You cannot see the beauty or the progress because you're comparing yourself to a man who started out with a perfect, beautiful yard in the first place. <u>The problem is we tend to compare our worst traits with the best traits in others.</u> This kind of correlation leads to extreme defeat, making us want to give up the healing journey completely.

Here's the beauty though. <u>Redemption shines brightest on the darkest of canvases. The little zinnia is proof of how far you've come. It may not seem like you've healed that much, but since you've had so much more to overcome than others, your redemption beams all that more</u>.

Stop trying to act like folks who never had sexual injury (Reference: Mary Demuth / Not Marked: Finding Hope and Healing After Sexual Abuse).

Do you know your value?

Proverbs 31:10: Charm is deceptive, and beauty is fleeting; but a woman who fears the LORD is to be praised (NIV).

Before we entered into the Kingdom and decided to fully surrender our lives to the Lord, we measured ourselves based on the world's scale. Every culture, every country, and every system has certain traits and qualities that they exalt over others. As a woman who ranked highly in the world, you have to intentionally humble yourself and choose to view yourself in a sober light. Measure yourself on the Kingdom scale and you will soar with confidence. Measure yourself on the world's scale and you will find yourself double-minded and unstable in all your ways. Doing this in our own strength is nearly impossible. All the same, we must ask God to teach us how to humble ourselves so that we can place our value in the eternal/internal, not the external qualities. God opposes the proud, but He gives grace to the humble. I can't speak on behalf of all women, but for me, once God opened my eyes to my own value, I looked in the mirror, and I could finally see physical beauty. Yes, it was God who opened my eyes to see that this tent that He placed His Spirit to dwell in was attractive, but this also created a lot of pride and entitlement inside of me. In the process of 'pursuing' the *man I loved,* I became pretty lost. Before I allowed him to take a greater place in my life than God, I was already walking on sinking sand.

> **1 Corinthians 13:11:** When I was a child, I talked like a child, I thought like a child, I reasoned like a child. When I became a man, I put the ways of childhood behind me (NIV).

In the past, Korean dramas, media, fashion, and music became the value system that I stood on. Yes, I was reading the bible *every* morning. Yes, I went to church *every* Sunday. Yet, the truth of the matter was that I was carnal and worldly. I felt *good* about myself *only* whenever I met the media's standard of beauty. By my senior year in college, I learned to do makeup, and I dyed my hair. By all means, I'm *not* saying that dying your hair and wearing makeup is sin, but my heart was not in the right place. I couldn't see myself as beautiful when I didn't have my contacts in. I saw myself as *better* and *more beautiful* than the other women around me whenever I mastered a certain look that was popular in media. This year, I decided to completely give up on secular music and Korean entertainment. This does not mean, I no longer like these things; it just means I outgrew them. I chose to lay aside the things I liked on His altar for greater joy and satisfaction in Him.

    As a woman thinketh, she is. When I no longer let Satan's voice ring in my ear, I began to hear God's voice more clearly. The Shepherd's' caring voice says my inner value is worth more than rubies and more precious than gold. Satan, the adversary's voice screams in my head that in order for me to be desirable, I must appeal to a man's carnality. When I no longer let media define my value, I'm able to see myself in a balanced view. The devil is a liar. If I have to win him by my carnality, I will have to keep him by my carnality.

Chapter 6

The Former Seductress Learns How to Guard Her Heart

At the time, my worship was in the *man I loved,* so I constantly compared myself to the women in the church who I thought he was interested in. By passively pursuing a man through prayer, I was losing myself. The spirit of rejection heavily manifested itself inside of me. Little did I know at the time that Satan was using me as a weapon formed against the *man I loved.*

> **Proverbs 7:10-15:** Then out came a woman to meet him, dressed like a prostitute and with crafty intent. (She is unruly and defiant, her feet never stay at home; now in the street, now in the squares, at every corner she lurks.) She took hold of him and kissed him

and with a brazen face she said:
"Today I fulfilled my vows, and I have food from my fellowship offering at home. So I came out to meet you;
I looked for you and have found you (NIV)!

Proverbs 7 depicts a seductress or, in other words, an adulteress. Cambridge dictionary states to seduce is "to **persuade** or cause **someone to do something that they would not usually consider** doing **by being very attractive** and difficult to refuse." A seductress is a woman who intentionally or unintentionally leads the men of God astray. We become distractions to the men in our lives when we use our lips, eyes, mouth, teeth, hair, breasts, hips, butt and thighs to lure men to ourselves. In my opinion, whenever we change our God-given personalities, whether outgoing or shy, in an attempt to win a man over, that is being a seductress.

What is your intention when you wear that short skirt that shows your behind when you bend over? What is your heart's motive when you wear that bright red lipstick? What is your intention when you dress a certain way?

The Former Seductress Learns How to Guard Her Heart

What is your intention when you speak certain words? Is it for attention?

It is OUT OF ORDER for a woman to pursue a man. Batting our eyelashes, dressing attractively, or changing our hairstyles for the purpose of getting a man's attention is a way of passively pursuing the man. Aggressively praying for a particular man to be with you is a form of pursuit. When you are praying against another person's will, this is a form of control. When a woman pursues a man, this is similar to a gazelle approaching a lion. The lion is confused and bewildered. When women pursue men, we discount ourselves. Men don't respect or take women seriously who pursue them. Don't be a silly woman.

When a particular man passively pursues a woman, he might walk in front of you and say *hey.* He might sit two rows ahead of you, but turn his head around and stare at you like a deer caught in headlights. He might buy a gift for you or do some other random acts of kindness. He might randomly give you an off-hand compliment one day. This man might just stare at you across the room and be too afraid to say hi. If this man happens to be attractive to you, it is easy for you, as a woman, to develop a story of how he is the love of your life and the two of you will end up on Bali beach together one day. The truth of the matter is he is interested in your interest. The more you respond to his passive pursuits, the more you will end up heartbroken. If a man does not make his intentions clear and known to you, he is NOT interested in you. Men are innate hunters. If a man is serious about you, you won't be left scratching your head and wondering, "What just happened here?" Let me repeat, sister, he is NOT interested. This particular man might just think you are cute or funny, but not wife material. Perhaps you remind him of his mother, and he has unresolved mother issues. In nine out of ten cases, this is a grown boy, and you are stroking his ego by responding to his passive pursuits. Ignore him and learn to say, "I got to go!" Then, throw on your running shoes and run. When Joseph encountered Potiphar's wife, what did he do? He fled! The reason you are attracting these kind of grown boys is because of the undelivered spirits inside of you. Your demons are attracting his demons.

The Former Seductress Learns How to Guard Her Heart

How does a woman guard her heart? She needs to guard her love language. There are five love languages: words of affirmation, gifts, acts of service, quality time, and physical touch. Intimacy is built through time and consistency. Satan deceived Eve. She gave him a measure of her quality time and she allowed him to speak words of deception into her. Not everyone deserves access to you. You wouldn't let a thief into your home, so why do you allow trash (demons in handsome flesh) into your life? At the first sight of a talking snake, she should've just put on her running shoes and fled. I will list my personal boundaries as an example. To note, what works for me may or may not work for you. Every woman needs to know herself well enough, so that she will enact personal boundaries to guard her heart. Pray and ask the Holy Spirit to help you make your own personal set of guidelines. For me, I don't spend one-on-one time with any member of the opposite gender. This ensures that I guard my quality time. I also don't allow a man to individually compliment me. If a man walks up to me and attempts to flatter me with words, he is in for a rude awakening. I quickly shut him down. "Thanks for saying I look nice, but I think

Janette looks nice as well." Then, I will physically turn away and walk in a different direction. This gives me the upper hand, because he does not gain individual access to me. I don't message men individually. For ministry purposes, I message men in group messages. For my married leaders, I make sure I include their wives' e-mail, so there isn't any room for any funny business. I also make sure to send a polite, "I hope you and your wife are doing well" as my way of displaying honor through acknowledgment. If a married man were to ever come up to me and complain to me about his wife, I will quickly shut him down and cease to contact him. I do not want to be an adulterous woman who splits up marriages. I do not allow a man to excessively talk to me about issues that are going on in his life on an individual basis. If he does attempt to tell me his issues, I quickly shut him down. "Have you talked to a brother about that? I'm a female. I'm not equipped to deal with your male issues." This is an example of what I would reply with. I don't let a man serve me. I make sure I pack light, so I don't need a man to help me with my bags. I don't let men hug me, touch me, or commit any other physical acts. I keep my legs closed. I don't let a man kiss me. If a man wants to individually see me, I will turn him down and offer a group alternative instead.

    As a single woman, you will have to say a lot of, "I go to go's," and that's okay. I do make exceptions for the boundaries I listed above. The Holy Spirit is my Counselor, so if the Holy Spirit alerts me that the man is saying this out of a fatherly heart, I will accept the compliment, but I will also quickly flee. I don't accept gifts from the opposite gender unless it's for special events such as birthdays where it's socially acceptable. I don't accept acts of service unless it's a general social custom such as men opening doors for women. An exception that I made recently to my boundaries was when I was with my female friend and one of her guy friends approached her. The Spirit of God gave me a word of knowledge about his family, and therefore, I shared about my brokenness from my family. I shared about how I was able to experience God's love. I also prayed for him to experience wholeness. He asked me for my social media contact. I politely refused. In this case, I almost broke *all* my rules. Yet, it was God's Spirit that led me to do so.

Every woman has her own individual weaknesses. I want to remind you. The opposite gender is not our enemy. The enemy is Satan.

> **Ephesians 6:12:** For we wrestle not against flesh and blood, but against principalities, against powers, against the rulers of the darkness of this world, against spiritual wickedness in high places (KJV).

As a woman who has had a history of lust, this is an area that I need to heavily be on guard.

> **1 Peter 5:8:** Be sober, be vigilant; because your adversary the devil, as a roaring lion, walketh about, seeking whom he may devour (KJV).

King David was a great leader, but Satan knew about his lusts, so he used Bathsheba as bait. Samson lusted after Delilah. In turn, he gave her the secrets to his great strength. His anointing came in the bundle of his locks. In the end, the Philistines gauged Samson's eyes out. Protect your anointing. God has set you apart for a reason, because He has a great call on your life. Do not sacrifice your anointing for a relationship. Your purpose in life is to build the Kingdom of God and to destroy the works of the enemy. If a man meets you along your journey to purpose, hallelujah! Praise the Lord! If this never happens, you are full and complete on your own. When God fills your voids and you become baptized with the Holy Ghost, there is an unspeakable peace and joy that indwells within your spirit. The longing for a man dies down, and at this stage of your life, the idea of a man seems like a burden, not a blessing. If a man is not an asset to your life, he is a deficit. You must have an overflowing emotional, mental, spiritual bank account by the time you are ready to be a wife. That way, when he deposits strength in you, it will be an addition to what you already possess. If he leaves, you won't be left famished for love, because you already have love within yourself. You might lose some emotional, mental, and spiritual resources, but you won't go bankrupt if he leaves. This also ensures that you have resources to give to him. The problem that I had was I refused to let go of the *man I loved* in spite of the red flags I saw; this was because I'd already invested two entire years of my life liking him. I also waited for him for an entire year to come back to America. I was a silly woman who did not heed to the fact that any wise business owner knows when to cut their losses. Perhaps, they lost $100,000, but it is even worse to wait another two years and lose an additional $500,000 dollars by staying in a toxic, unhealthy situation.

The main issue with women is that we allow men to give us what we won't give ourselves. As an example, when I was in East Asia, I interned at an advertising company during the summer of my junior year. I developed a huge crush on my boss just from his one act of kindness. He bought me pizza from Pizza Hut on the first day behind the set. As you can clearly see, I had been starved from love, since I was a child. He tickled my fancy. When you have been abused, broken, battered, and mishandled by your family, it is your responsibility to fill up your own gaping wounds. Yes, there is God, but God helps those who help themselves. Faith without works is dead.

Practically speaking, this entails learning to invest in yourself. You are a valuable stock.

Don't be stingy on money, otherwise, if a man comes like a dog with his tongue out begging you for a treat, you will give yourself away. You won't be easily impressed by anything a man offers you if you value and invest in yourself. Go on expensive dates with God. Date yourself and God as a single woman. Buy yourself that expensive name brand bag and gold jewelry. Buy yourself flowers. What are the things you have planned on doing with the man of God of your dreams? Is it watching sunsets on a beach, going to a record store and listening to your favorite tunes, laying on the grass and gazing up at the stars? Listen to me, sister, you can do all the romantic, fantastical things with God.

> **Isaiah 54:5:** <u>For your Maker is your husband</u>-- the LORD Almighty is his name-- the Holy One of Israel is your Redeemer; he is called the God of all the earth (NIV).

One of the husband's roles is to financially provide for his wife. In our home, my father failed to financially provide for his family, so my mother lost all respect for him. Fortunately, God is a good husband. God has given you money for a reason. The Bible tells us to love others as we love **ourselves.** It's kind of hard to love others with a pure motive, not to brown-nose, if we simply don't love ourselves. It is human nature to value what we invest in. When you spend money on yourself, you will find yourself more valuable. In my life, I was always stingy on treating myself to nice meals. I figured that when I met my man of God, he would take me out to all of my favorite restaurants. Every time I went to a restaurant, I would pick the cheapest thing on the menu. Now, I don't do that anymore. When I was first getting over the *man I loved,* I scheduled a Father (God) and daughter date every week. I went to a pretty café and I got dressed up, even though I felt like a fool at first. This was because I was actively practicing filling up the hole in my heart. During the date with God, I just sat there and poured my heart out, and He met me there every single time.

During my first two years in the field, I wanted desperately to reconnect with the *man I loved.* I knew he wasn't good for me. I had seen the red flags. Yet, I was starved for affection and love. In my family of origin, I was always the one listening to everyone else's problems. No one listened to me. When *the man I loved* came around, I would type long paragraphs about my life on messenger, even though he would only reply on occasion. I felt loved. I felt like he listened and cared. The problem with me was that I talked too much. My love language is words of affirmation. In spite of the words being on the computer screen, whenever he did get around to reply with, "God has a good plan for your life," it melted my heart.

> In The Female Brain, published in 2006, Louann Brizendine, M.D. claimed that women say about 20,000 words a day, while men say about 7,000. (Reference: Psychology Today, Do Women Really Talk More Than Men).

The problem with women is we desire to be heard by everyone we encounter. We demand attention like a two-year-old crying in a corner because she didn't get her way. As a single woman, learn to talk nonstop in the presence of God. He hears you. He knows you. He loves you. When a guy who is quiet and passive approaches you, you won't feel the need to talk nonstop. Learn to be absolutely naked in front of God. Like you would strip naked in front of your future spouse, strip naked in front of God. Let God know all your weaknesses, vulnerabilities, secret sins, hurts, and the deepest parts of your heart. When Adam and Eve ate from the Tree of the Knowledge of Good and Evil, they covered up their shame with fig leaves. Be unashamed with God. Tell God your secrets, things you wouldn't even tell your closest friends. This is good practice because you have exercised your talking muscles in front of our great God. By the time a man comes along, you won't feel the need to tell all your childhood abuse to this man, making him into a therapist, because you have already processed your pain.

> **2 Timothy 3:6:** For of this sort are they which creep into houses, and lead captive <u>silly women</u> laden with sins, led away with divers lusts (KJV).

Don't be a silly women! These women are full of voids and full of futile desires. Take your desires to the Lord. Pray and ask God to fill up your voids. A man walking into your life and showing you the slightest bit of attention and affection won't have room to set up his couch, soda, and chips in the space of your heart if you won't make room for him. If your heart is full of the Holy Spirit and your mind is sober, you are a strong woman.

> *Lord, may you take way this woman's foolish desires and let her find life by walking with you. Let thine eye be single on you. Fill her cup up, make it whole, so she thirsts no more. Give her a sober mind. A mind that is obsessed and infatuated with you. In Jesus Name, Amen* (Psalm 119:37, CEV).

It is foolish for a woman in this day and age to assume that she will get married.
Elisabeth Elliot, a female missionary, says it this way:

> "I beg women to wait. Wait on God. **Keep your mouth shut.** Don't expect anything until the declaration is clear and forthright. And to the men I say be careful with us, please. Be circumspect."

> "Unless a man is prepared to ask a woman to be his wife, what right has he

to claim her exclusive attention? **Unless she has been asked to marry him, why would a sensible woman promise any man her exclusive attention?** If, when the time has come for a commitment, he is not man enough to ask her to marry him, she should give him no reason to presume that she belongs to him" (Reference: Passion & Purity).

The biggest battle for a woman begins in her mind. Be sober minded. Do not entertain fantasy. If you find a man attractive, acknowledge it in your head and move on. Do not entertain and meditate about a man day-in and day-out. When I was a nonbeliever, every encounter with an attractive man led me to fantasize and create a script in my head. I would dream about when, where, and how this handsome man and I would meet again. This guy could be a sales clerk at H&M, but because I didn't know my value, I would imagine him whisking me away from all my problems. As you could see, I was not done processing my pain at the time. That handsome sales clerk is NOT your husband. Just because he smiled at you and waved at you doesn't mean he is interested in you. That cute boy at church is NOT your husband. Use your brain, sister. Cut off the soap operas that make you feel sorry for being single and your lack of a functional family. Stop listening to that secular music that tells you that you are all by yourself and that your body is an object for men to use. That's a lie from the pit of hell. When you became a follower of Christ, the Holy Spirit was deposited in you. Do not grieve the Spirit by ignoring His presence. He lives inside of you. You are never alone because you have the Spirit of God.

How can any sensible woman presume anyone to be her husband if he has not *even* actively pursued her? Active pursuit is when a man makes his intentions clear that he wants to enter into a courtship with you. Don't allow your heart to get ahead of your head. If you 'must' like him, please just like him in the realm of your mind. I "think" he is an attractive man. I "think" he would make a great husband. Those are just passing thoughts. Do not mediate on them. Whatever you do, do not let this man get into the crevices of your heart. When you let these thoughts go to the realm of the heart, you must cast it out. Whatever you don't cast down, you must cast out. If after three months, he still has not pursued you, drop him like a hot bag of bricks.

Chapter 7

Building Your Own Self-Worth and the Three Virgins

You have to have dreams outside of marriage. If your biggest dream in life is to get married, you have made marriage into an idol. The highest point of your existence is to do God's will. This should shake up your bones and excite you. Practically speaking, ask God to give you dreams outside of marriage. Do not put all your eggs in one basket. If you put all your hope in marriage, you will be severely disappointed. Get around married people who aren't afraid to tell you the hardships and realities that marriage entails. Are you ready to wash a man's dirty, crusty underwear? Are you ready to lie next to a pair of thighs that haven't showered for days? These are some of the realities of marriage. Marriage isn't a fairy tale; it's hard work. If responsibility and commitment scares you, then you aren't ready. Marriage is ministry. Your ministry should begin before you get married, and continue after God unites you with your king. Your ministry is to spread the gospel and to make disciples of all nations. Take your time and allow God to grow you up to become a woman of God. After God grows you up to become a woman, He will grow you to become a wife. When you become a wife, He then hides you. When God hides you, this is a blessing. He who finds a **wife,** finds a good thing. You must become a wife before you are a wife. Even when you are hidden, you might be hidden for many years. All your friends might get married before you. This usually means that God has special assignments for you to complete in singleness. That's okay. You are a queen and God has prepared a king for you. Don't settle for anyone less.

Women need to have a solid plan outside of marriage. This sounds like common sense, but the reality is that you <u>might not</u> get married. You cannot hope that your knight in shining armor or Jesus in handsome flesh will come to whisk you away from your financial woes or other emotional mishaps (loneliness, insecurity, boredom, fear, lust, addiction, etc). For the women who grew up without proper fathers in your lives, you must be *even* more on guard and discerning. There are many false prophets within the church. You cannot assume that the boy with shiny church shoes, speaking tongues of fire, and raising his hands in the front pews is a man of God. Tiffany Buckner, a deliverance minister, puts it this way, "Is he saved, sanctified, and filled with the Holy Ghost?" Sanctification ensures that he has the character to withhold his anointing, and he is not just a carnal babe in Christ full of spiritual gifts, lacking in real revelation, wisdom, and love.

> **Mark 16:17:** And these signs will accompany those who believe: in my name they will cast out demons; they will speak in new tongues (ESV).

It will be hard to submit to a weak-willed, fleshly man. Your leaders are your covering. They are similar to shields that the enemy hits with his darts so they can't get to you. If God does send you a husband, your future husband will be your spiritual covering. Imagine submitting to a man who does not exercise his spiritual authority. (I hear the sound of crickets chirping in the background.) This is the sound of dismay. It is asinine to marry a man that you cannot respect. A weak fleshly man like Ahab will not be able to cover a powerful queen like you.

    We attract who we are. Tony Gaskins, a prominent relationship coach, describes it this way, "Brain, body, and brand." If you are a broken woman, you will attract a broken man. Work on yourself so that you will be a blessing to your future husband as well. If God sends us powerful men of God, we want to be powerful women of God. Find out ways you can make extra streams of revenue. Has God given you any ideas? Don't be afraid to pursue them. A powerful man of God will be bored if all you have to talk about is makeup, clothes, and hair. Educate yourself about the events of this world. Go on mission trips. Write a book. Build a business. Build an orphanage. Start a non-profit. Get a PhD. Invest in missionaries. Support a child. Travel the world. Buy your own house. These are just a few ideas. Work on your physical health. Does diabetes or other health conditions run in your family? Change your diet, because you want a long life to serve our God. Work out for your physical well-being. Take care of your hygiene. Don't walk around with foul body odor. Do you have a clean home? If it looks like a pig inhabits your space, create a consistent cleaning schedule. These are some ideas. God will give you more if you ask.

Be the change that you want to see. You are not a victim, but a survivor. The same spirit that raised Jesus from the dead is the same spirit that lives in you. After reading the pages above, you might see yourself as a victim of trauma. I beseech you, sister, please go to a Christian therapist, get deliverance, and seek wholeness in God.

In a society of masculinized women and feminized men, women have taken on the role of the pursuer. In this day and age, there are more opportunities for women in ministry, work, and education. I beseech you, sister. Do not pursue any man. You are the prize. God brought Eve to Adam. It was not the other way around. When you bring something to someone, it is usually a gift. A gift is very valuable. He was presenting a valuable gift to Adam. Sister, you are the gift. It was Adam who needed a helpmeet. Adam needed Eve. You don't need Adam. Get that knowledge into your pretty head. A **wo**man is a man with a **wo**mb. Women are meant to multiply, increase, and give birth. Although as a single woman, you cannot give birth to physical children, you have the precious gift of birthing spiritual children. Isn't that precious? You also have the ability to birth businesses, inventions, and ideas. You can also help orphans and help those who are less fortunate than you are. Don't limit yourself to a man. Don't spend your single years waiting on a man to rescue you. Be your own superman. Put on your big girl pants and get to plowing. You cannot be a helpmeet if you cannot first help yourself. You cannot help your future husband if you remain crippled and helpless. Be the powerful woman of God that you are. Stand firm in your authority. The harvest is plentiful, but the workers are few.

Matthew 25 illustrates the parable of the ten virgins.

> **Matthew 25:1-13:** "At that time the kingdom of heaven will be like ten virgins who took their lamps and went out to meet the bridegroom. Five of them were foolish and five were wise.

The foolish ones took their lamps but did not take any oil with them. The wise ones, however, took oil in jars along with their lamps. The bridegroom was a long time in coming, and they all became drowsy and fell asleep.

"At midnight the cry rang out: 'Here's the bridegroom! Come out to meet him!'

"Then all the virgins woke up and trimmed their lamps. The foolish ones said to the wise, 'Give us some of your oil; our lamps are going out.'

"'No,' they replied, 'there may not be enough for both us and you. Instead, go to those who sell oil and buy some for yourselves.'

"But while they were on their way to buy the oil, the bridegroom arrived. The virgins who were ready went in with him to the wedding banquet. And the door was shut.

"Later the others also came. 'Lord, Lord,' they said, 'open the door for us!'

"But he replied, 'Truly I tell you, I don't know you.'

"Therefore keep watch, because you do not know the day or the hour (NIV).

In ancient Israel, traditionally, the fathers arranged marriage. Fathers met with other fathers to discuss the details in regard to the contractual agreement. If the fathers agreed to have their children betrothed, the children would marry when they became adults. Upon agreement, they had the engagement ceremony at the woman's house. The bridegroom must bring a gift to the brides' house. This is the bride price. He is purchasing her. The father needed to be sure that this man could provide for his daughter's needs. In those days, engagement was almost equal to marriage. Unlike modern times, there was protocol and order back then. These days, any perverted male on the street can approach a woman, lick his lips, and harass her. In ancient times, the father acted as protection. The bridegroom, after preparing the gift, went back to his father's house to prepare a room for the bride. The bridegroom went home and it took a year until he was completely ready. All the while, the bride prepared herself to be a wife. During this time, she purified herself for her husband. She was in *preparation.* The woman spent time with her family learning how to be a wife and how to cook. She learned to keep herself holy. The bride didn't know the exact time or date her bridegroom would arrive. Unfortunately, in modern times, Satan has taken the father out of many women's lives. The father is either a deadbeat, absent, unavailable, or abusive. Women with these kind of men as fathers need to have older men in their lives to examine the men that come into their lives. Even for the most masculine woman, a male perspective always proves to be helpful in these cases.

Let's take the three virgins who were waiting for their husbands and put this in modern context. To my sisters who have lost their virginity in the world: you are a born-again virgin in God's eyes. Envision this. Three women are waiting for their God-ordained husbands. They all wait with different attitudes and varying level of faiths.

Virgin 1: This woman serves at church, but is religious. She is a Pharisee and she thinks her dirty rags of good works can earn her a spouse. She gives the stank eye to other women in the congregation. She looks in disdain at the married women. Her heart is full of jealousy and comparison. When her friends get engaged, she does not celebrate with them, instead she mourns on the inside. One day, she catches a cute new guy at the congregation she serves at. He approaches her, but then he quickly walks away and rushes to the woman standing behind her. This woman steams with jealously. "How can he go after someone like her? I'm so much prettier than her!" On the flip side, she might think, "It's because I'm ugly. It's because I'm broken. That's why he didn't pick me." Every night, she prays to God about the cute new guy in the congregation. She bemoans and questions God. "How dare he pick someone like her?" or "Why am I not good enough for him?"

"Where's my husband, God?" cries the woman.

The problem with Virgin 1 is that she hasn't fully surrendered her life to God. She needs to allow God to be Lord in all areas of her life. She still has her plans, her dreams, and her ideals for her life. Perhaps, this woman has had a hard and challenging past. She struggles with rejection, rebellion, pride, insecurity, jealousy, worldliness, isolation, and/or a poverty mindset. This woman often has trust issues, so she lives in her own caves. She doesn't know her own value. She is insecure, so she becomes jealous. This woman is measuring her value based on the world's scale and not the Kingdom's scale. She spends more time in the mirror and less time working on her inner man. She will attract a worldly man if she keeps walking down this road. In order for her to heal, she must let God take her through a difficult process of dying to self. As she dies to self through serving others, God will purify her motives. She will also have to take active steps of faith and seek the help she needs. This process requires vulnerability, and that is scary. Help might come through therapists, deliverance ministers, mentors, and/or counselors. When she does encounter these people, she must honor her way through each relationship. Honor helps her receive the impartation that God wants to bestow upon her through them. Yes, she will be offended. She will be tempted to run. Despite these obstacles, she has to value her freedom more than her fear. She has to learn the value of commitment, even through offense. She has to make it up in her mind that she won't quit on people because of her devotion to God. As she heals, gets to know God's heart, God will reveal her purpose to her. This is when she rises up to become the queen that she is.

Virgin 2: This woman grew up in a Christian home. If she didn't grow up in a Christian home, she had relatively healthy parental units. Her parents are either white-collar workers or missionaries/pastors. This woman turns 30. She might have a nine to five job. She is tired of being single. She voices her displeasure to her friends, family, and pastor. All she talks about is her single status. She allows society to be her voice. Society says that she's running out of time. The enemy hears her heart, too. The enemy smells her desperation.

A man approaches her one-day. This man isn't saved, sanctified, or filled with the Holy Spirit. He is "Christian" though. All the same, she is not attracted to him. There is no connection, but she is tired of waiting on God. She is twiddling her thumbs, desperate for a man. She sees that her cousin is in a relationship. She feels the biological clock ticking. The pressure is on. She accepts the proposition of the man. "Why not?" she says to herself. It is better to be in a relationship than to be single. I'm running out of time, and I want to give birth to my own children. Later, she becomes married to a man who turns out to have an unresolved porn addiction. He spends all his time watching pornography, while she is cradling two crying newborns.

The problem with Virgin 2 is that she hasn't discovered her value outside of her connection with her parents and society. She still defines her value based on who she is connected to. This woman has spent all her life living to what culture has confined her to be. She hasn't discovered who she really is because she has spent all her life living for the expectations of others. Yes, she is loyal to God, but she lacks a genuine and intimate connection with Him. In order to discover who she is, she must begin seeking first the Kingdom of God. She must be willing to shatter the expectations of her parents, peers, and society. She must learn to have her own voice and opinions. Her unnatural obsession with children might stem from the fact that she had a poor mother. Her mother may have been not the nurturing kind. She longs to give her kids the love and nurture she has never received from her mother or for herself. She needs to allow God to heal her from her mother wounds, so she can be an effective mother. Otherwise, she will try to live vicariously through her children.

Virgin 3: This woman has gone through the process of dying to self. She has had to mourn and come to peace with her upbringing. She has had to die her way out of bad relationships and situations she once placed herself in. She has had to break away from many toxic mindsets and lies. She has had to humble herself time and time again, so she could receive deliverance. She is aware that she has come far along her journey. Despite it all, she intentionally and aggressively humbles herself, so she doesn't give a foothold to the enemy. When she was an unbeliever, she was heavily entrenched in the world's doctrine. The world's music, way of dress, and way of speech guided her footsteps. She was a slave to the world. Upon God opening her eyes, she began to see her value. Her inherent value is in her status as God's daughter. Now, she is determined to

destroy the works of the enemy. She exposes her own past, so she can set others free.
This woman sees herself in a balanced light: a beautiful, talented, demon-slaying, princess warrior of God, yet, also a flawed and imperfect woman in much need of a Savior. She sees that the beauty, prowess, knowledge, and skill she possesses are all because of her God. She praises Him for she is wonderfully made. She is also aware that her flaws don't define her, but they only make her human. When she is rebuked, although she feels offense rise up, she humbly receives it. She knows that she is not perfect, nor is she trying to be. She walks in confidence because she knows the one in whom her confidence lies. She is willing to lose the approval of people for the approval of God. Yes, she has her issues that she has not yet overcome. She is aware of them and is taking active measures to get the help she needs. This woman wrestles down offense. She also contains her emotions until she reaches her prayer closet at home. She has learned to speak only when the Spirit leads and when mature revelation bubbles from her belly. She has learned to hear the voice of God. This woman also is aware she has not arrived. There is always more room to grow.

Building Your Own Self-Worth and the Three Virgins

This woman is no longer a lost daughter. She has become a hidden one. She knows that God has prepared an awesome, demon-slaying, world-changing, attractive man of God for her. Yet, she is not waiting for him to show up at her doorstep anytime soon. She is too busy building God's Kingdom to wait on a man to show up. Yes, she is still a woman. She still has longings and desires. She surrenders them to His feet. She is honest about her emotions, and she doesn't hide them from God, after all, God already sees them. She makes her desires clear to God, surrendered with an open hand. Not my will, but thy will be done. Her life's verse is, "Seek first the Kingdom of God and all its righteousness, and all these things will be added onto thee."

How will you wait during your single years? Will you wait with a jealous and impatient heart, unwilling to celebrate your other sisters? Will you let the unresolved issues in your heart fester? Will you settle for any man who comes knocking at your door?

If you allow God to, He can develop you into a confident, fearless woman of God. When you walk in the room, demons will tremble because they know that you know your Maker.

Chapter 8

Attraction in the Kingdom Language

Fear is perverted faith. It's faith in and towards Satan's kingdom. Many young women, myself included, struggle with the notion that God will send us an undesirable and unattractive mate. In Song of Solomon 1:16, the sister who has been darkened by the sun declares, "How handsome you are, my beloved." The woman who has been darkened by the sun physically perceives that her betrothed is physically attractive. She finds him visually stimulating to *her* eyes.

Arguably speaking, beauty is in the eye of the beholder. Beauty is also a social and cultural constraint. What is appealing to the majority of the population is what is commonly propagated through the television screen, billboards, and other media outlets. Anyone found in the outlier group is deemed 'ugly' or unattractive by the masses. This is the world's definition of beauty. I too have wrestled with what I should look for in a potential spouse. When I was a double-minded believer, I held a list of shallow standards that my future husband had to meet in order for him to even qualify for a date with me.

As a single Asian-American woman, I was once bound by Korean dramas and entertainment. Korean dramas depicted the ideal man to be around six feet tall, skinny (yet well built), pale with nicely styled hair, and he has feminine facial features as a bonus additive. This was what I considered as beautiful, sexy, and attractive. Any man who fell outside of my 'type,' I characterized him as 'ugly.' Every culture has a different definition of what beauty is. Fortunately, the mind is flexible and bendable. It can be trained to appreciate different kinds of physicality. With the help of the Holy Spirit, our Counselor, we can learn to find men in all kinds and shapes of tents to be attractive.

Attraction can possibly begin through the eyes, but can also be built over time. I compare the process of attraction with an artist layering watercolors on a piece of paper. The artist has to wait for each color to dry completely before layering another color. The colors become more vibrant as she waits for the layer to completely dry; this is before adding another layer of color. If the artist adds a layer of paint before it dries completely, the color will bleed out and the likeliness of spottiness will increase. Attraction is similar to the waiting period for paint to dry. It can take an incredulous amount of time for the colors to vibrantly melt on the canvas, but it's well worth the wait.

In a microwave culture, many young women do not like to wait. We want life to come in a nicely prepackaged instant meal that heats up at a moment's notice. This includes our desire for attraction to be instantly obtained. As an example, this kind of attraction is equivalent to locking eyes with a handsome stranger across the room. Sweaty palms, racing heart, and butterflies might emerge as a result of this quick encounter. The challenge against this mindset is to be open to the possibility that God may or may not grant you instantaneous physical attraction towards your future spouse. The attraction God might give you may take time to cook and stew, just like a good home-cooked meal.

Young women are taught that attraction must begin at "You caught me at hello" or the classic "Love at first sight." This is what Hollywood and other popular cultures teach young women. This love at first sight or, in better words, *lust at first glance*, is solely based on pheromones or biological chemistry. Certain perfumes function in the same way as certain scents; they blend well with our inherent body chemistry. In short, we can be carnally attracted to certain types of men.

We definitely cannot build a relationship *purely* based on physical attraction. Physical attraction is like the poles of the magnets that pull towards each other, but Godly character is what causes us to stay. When a relationship is solely built on attraction, this is equivalent to building a house on sinking sand, rather than a solid foundation. When the storms of life come, the house will disintegrate into a thousand pieces. Love is the foundation for a healthy and sustainable relationship. Passion without love is lust. Yet, if there is absolutely no attraction for a sustained period of time, it's wise to prayerfully consider terminating the courtship. It is unfair for the pursuer to pour all his eggs into one basket (you), while you are keeping him around due to loneliness, boredom, fear, or insecurity.

Unfortunately, society sets a double standard for women. In the world, we are taught that men are the prize and women should be grateful that a man would approach them and ask for their numbers. For women who have yet awakened to their inherent value and worth, a man can prove to be exciting and life-changing. "Oh wowzers, a man approached me! I must be valuable!" exclaims the woman. This could be far from true. For her value is not in a man approaching her or choosing her, her value is in the fact that God chose her before the beginning of time and she is His daughter. If the idea of a man rejecting you throws you off course, chances are, you have unprocessed childhood rejection. **Ephesians 1:6 (KJV):** To the praise of the glory of his grace, wherein he hath made us accepted in the beloved. Remember, we are accepted in the beloved.

An unfair double standard is placed on women. The classic line spewed by society is that men are visual creatures. Therefore, women are blind. This puts unnecessary pressure on the woman to accept any suitor who comes strolling her way for the fear of appearing shallow in front of her peers. It is quite abominable when a man continues to pursue a woman in spite of her firm rejections. No means no. His narcissistic badgering might cause her to collapse under pressure and accept his proposition. Little does this young man know, he might get her to the altar, but he won't have her heart.

In Genesis 11, a tower of Babel was being built. At first, the world spoke a common tongue. When they attempted to build a tower that reached the heavens, God scattered them and the people no longer understood one another. For young women, our potential suitors' faces might be put in a completely different language, and we don't have the right tools to decipher them. In order to understand their faces better, we must ask God for wisdom and the heart to understand. If after much prayerful consideration, we still do not feel the Spirit of God changing our hearts and there aren't any other qualities that draw us to our suitors, we are possibly courting someone else's husband. It is best to let these guys go, so they can move on with their lives. To be transparent, I'm not in a position to court anyone at this time because I still prefer to be highly attracted to my spouse physically. This displays a level of immaturity, and it shows that I need more individual time with the Lord, so that He can develop my character. In short, preferences are *not* bad. Preferences become toxic when we idolize them. In the end, it's not my will, but God's will be done.

There are four facets of attraction; they are: physical, emotional, spiritual, and mental. As a Kingdom believer, I am challenged to see beyond what meets my eye and to look deeper. Isaiah said this about Jesus, "For he grew up before him like a young plant, and like a root out of dry ground; **he had no form or majesty that we should look at him, and no beauty that we should desire him**" (Isaiah 53:2 ESV). The psychological components of attraction are listed below:

> What do you think is the single most influential factor in determining with

whom you become friends and whom you form romantic relationships? You might be surprised to learn that the answer is simple: the people with whom you have the most contact. This most important factor is proximity. You are more likely to be friends with people you have regular contact with. For example, there are decades of research that shows that you are more likely to become friends with people who live in your dorm, your apartment building, or your immediate neighborhood than with people who live farther away (Festinger, Schachler, & Back, 1950). It is simply easier to form relationships with people you see often because you have the opportunity to get to know them.

One of the reasons why proximity matters to attraction is that it breeds familiarity; people are more attracted to that which is familiar. Just being around someone or being repeatedly exposed to them increases the likelihood that we will be attracted to them. We also tend to feel safe with familiar people, as it is likely we know what to expect from them. Dr. Robert Zajonc (1968) labeled this phenomenon the mere-exposure effect. More specifically, he argued that the more often we are exposed to a stimulus (e.g., sound, person) the more likely we are to view that stimulus positively. Moreland and Beach (1992) demonstrated this by exposing a college class to four women (similar in appearance and age) who attended different numbers of classes, revealing that the more classes a woman attended, the more familiar, similar, and attractive she was considered by the other students.

There is a certain comfort in knowing what to expect from others; consequently, research suggests that we like what is familiar. While this is often on a subconscious level, research has found this to be one of the most basic principles of attraction (Zajonc, 1980). For example, a young man growing up with an overbearing mother may be attracted to other overbearing women not because he likes being dominated but rather because it is what he considers normal (i.e., familiar).

Similarity is another factor that influences who we form relationships with. We are more likely to become friends or lovers with someone who is similar to us in background, attitudes, and lifestyle. In fact, there is no evidence that opposites attract. Rather, we are attracted to people who are most like us (Figure 1) (McPherson, Smith-Lovin, & Cook, 2001). Why do you think we are attracted to people who are similar to us? Sharing things in common will certainly make it easy to get along with others and form connections. When you and another person share similar music taste, hobbies, food preferences, and so on, deciding what to do with your time together might be easy. Homophily is the tendency for people to form social networks, including friendships, marriage, business relationships, and many other types of relationships, with others who are similar (McPherson et al., 2001).

People tend to be attracted to similar people. Many couples share a cultural background. This can be quite obvious in a ceremony such as a wedding, and more subtle (but no less significant) in the day-to-day workings of a relationship. (credit: modification of work by Shiraz Chanawala)

But, homophily limits our exposure to diversity (McPherson et al., 2001). By forming relationships only with people who are similar to us, we will have homogenous groups and will not be exposed to different points of view. In other words, because we are likely to spend time with those who are most like ourselves, we will have limited exposure to those who are different than ourselves, including people of different races, ethnicities, social-economic status, and life situations.

Once we form relationships with people, we desire reciprocity. Reciprocity is the give and take in relationships. We contribute to relationships, but we expect to receive benefits as well. That is, we want our relationships to be a two-way street. We are more likely to like and engage with people who like us back. Self-disclosure is part of the two-way street. Self-disclosure is the sharing of personal information (Laurenceau, Barrett, & Pietromonaco, 1998). We form more intimate connections with people with whom we disclose important information about ourselves. Indeed, self-disclosure is a characteristic of healthy intimate relationships, as long as the information disclosed is consistent with our own views (Cozby, 1973) (Reference: Lumen Learning/ Forming Relationships).

Chapter 9

Lust of the Flesh, Lust of the Eyes, and the Pride of Life

As demonstrated above, attraction is multi-faceted and can be developed over time. To be transparent, the desire for my future mate to be culturally beautiful stems from three voids. I am not perfect, so I still struggle in these areas from time to time. It is a daily surrender that I put on the altar: the pride of life, lust of the eyes, and lust of the flesh. Paul advises his mentee, young Timothy, to flee from youthful lusts (2 Timothy 2:22, NIV).

> *Flee the evil desires of youth and pursue righteousness, faith, love and peace, along with those who call on the Lord out of a pure heart.*

I cannot claim that these are the same mindsets that have kept you bound, but I hope my struggles will help you find freedom from your chains.

> **1 John 2:15-2:16:**
> Do not love the world or anything in the world. If anyone loves the world, love for the Father is not in them.
> For everything in the world – the lust of the flesh, the lust of the eyes, and the pride of life – comes not from the Father but from the world (NIV).

As the verse above states, it is important to not love the world. When one chooses to worship the world, they become an enemy to God and a friend of Satan. They then choose to live their lives as double-minded believers, and Satan often torments their minds. To continue to live in between two systems, the Kingdom's system and the world's system, is *not* sustainable long term. Eventually, one of the systems will override the other system. When you first become a believer, the grace of the Lord abounds. Our heavenly Father gives us time to metaphorically tear off our old clothes and put on a new set. After a period of time, God starts disciplining us and He tests us to see if we prove to be faithful. There is a temptation for trauma survivors to pull the victim card out and choose to live in sin because of entitlement. For example, I used to tell God that I can sin, because I was in emotional pain. During those seasons, I let the enemy have a foothold in my life by continuing to ride between two systems of darkness and light. It's only when I chose to go all out for Christ that I experienced true freedom and peace. It's better to be hot or cold, rather than lukewarm.

1). *Lust of the Flesh*

According to the Macarthur Study Bible, the term flesh refers to the sin nature of man. The Greek word for flesh (sarx) is the rebellious self dominated by sin, and is often presented as a power in direct opposition to the Spirit.

When we become believers, we should desire to do the Father's will. Our spirit inside of us longs to please God, but our flesh the old nature is a slave to sin. We must choose to bare the yoke of righteousness and put to death our old nature. This consists of a tedious process of dying to ourselves; this is called sanctification. Sanctification begins in how we live our daily lives. Everyday, we have a choice to make; that is, to live for the Father or live for the enemy.

The mind plays an integral role in how the flesh will respond. If we allow our minds to be ruled by our flesh, we will die. Due to the mercy of God, we most likely won't physically die at the precise moment when we gratify our flesh, but we will end up quenching the Holy Spirit, and therefore, momentarily losing the internal peace, one of the fruits of the spirit (Romans 8:6). In order to develop a sound mind, a process of renewing and transforming of the mind takes place. The believer chooses to set (focus) his or her mind on what pleases the Father. This takes deliberate intentionality on the believer's part to call fire down from Heaven and bind particular thoughts that do not bring glory to God.

Our minds are like fertile soil. Thoughts are like seeds. Intense concentration on a particular thought creates thought patterns. Thought patterns are similar to the rain that pours down on the fertile soil. Thought patterns result in belief systems. Belief systems are the roots formed after much rain is poured down on the soil, resulting in a lush, green garden or a field of weeds. As an example of this analogy, I'll use myself. In the past, I would often encounter men who I found to be physically beautiful. I watered the seeds by continuously thinking about those men. Eventually, those seeds led to heavy rain or thought patterns. A simple encounter turned into a Disney movie where my knight in shining armor would rescue me, the damsel in distress. This often led to a stronghold where I firmly believed that the handsome men in question could be the Tylenol to my severe bleeding.

> **Galatians 5:19-21:** The acts of the flesh are obvious: sexual immorality, impurity and debauchery; idolatry and witchcraft; hatred, discord, jealousy, fits of rage, selfish ambition, dissensions, factions and envy; drunkenness, orgies, and the like. I warn you, as I did before, that those who live like this will not inherit the kingdom of God (NIV).

When the pursuit of happiness and pleasure drives our lives, there is a tendency to seek after these various acts of the flesh listed

Lust of the Flesh, Lust of the Eyes, and the Pride of Life

above. Sexual immorality is one of the most evident and unspoken killers of our soul. Unspoken refers to the fact that it is often socially taboo to strike up a conversation about sex. Often, I find that young women in the church who struggle with sexual sin are left silently suffering in the pews. In my case, sexual sin such as pornography and masturbation were sins that I had to overcome. These particular addictions affected how I viewed sexuality between a man and woman. As a younger woman who was thoroughly entrenched by the world's doctrine, I worshiped my own body and the pursuit of pleasure. As a survivor of childhood sexual abuse from the hands of my own biological father, I attempted to find ways out of the emotional turmoil that accompanied my pain by creating a fantasy world. As a result, I became addicted to the euphoric high that briefly followed the sexual act that was committed between my own hands and reproductive organs. In reality, the euphoric high never outlasted the shame I felt. After each attempt to escape my emotional turmoil, I was left feeling violated and naked; these were the same emotions I experienced when my father crossed my physical boundaries to satiate his lusts. This is perhaps the same shame Adam and Eve experienced when they attempted to use fig leaves to cover up their reproductive organs after disobeying God.

    As a survivor of childhood sexual abuse, I later became addicted to sexual immorality through the means of pornography and masturbation. Since the act of sex was introduced to my life at an early age, I was prematurely sexualized. Sexual perversion runs in my bloodline, so naturally, I became addicted to sex. When I became a Christian, upon entering undergrad, I was not fully delivered from these sins. I felt like a hypocrite who went to church on Sundays, yet, wrestled with the spirit of perversion during the weekday. Eventually, God led me to confide in two sisters in Christ. This was the beginning of my deliverance journey. Throughout the following years, it was an up and down journey of accountability, falling into sin, having breakthroughs, falling again, getting back up, and crying out for His mercy that led me to full deliverance. At first, this was merely an outward posture of obedience, thus, I became quite prideful. I boasted in my weeks of clean records with an occasional slip-up. It was only when God gave me a new heart and mind that outward obedience became an inward manifestation of the spirit. **Ezekiel 36:26:** And I will give you a new heart, and I will put a new spirit in you. I will take out your stony, stubborn heart and give you a tender, responsive heart (NLT). I now recognize that deliverance from sin is a gift from God, and any good fruit that comes out of my deliverance is not something I can boast in. *What we are delivered from is what God calls us to deliver.*

The shame that follows sexual sin is a reminder to the human that sex without love is vile in the eyes of God. Once again, sex without love is lust. Sexual immorality is a sin. In the Garden of Eden, the first act of sex occurred. The act of sex occurred in the proper context, therefore, it was honorable and pleased God. The term context refers to being in the right "sequence, connection, or setting." We serve a God of structure and order. In Genesis, the book that accounts for creation and design, there was a certain sequence that God orchestrated upon creating our world. The problem is when we choose a spouse before maturation, we pick based on what we were previously exposed to and our voids. What our flesh is exposed to before we became Christians often becomes a stronghold in our lives that we refer to as our 'type.' Our type, as women, tends to come in the flesh of the last man who walked out of our lives. This type often becomes a mandate we place before God demanding Him to give us our desires. Instead, we have to surrender to God on a daily basis until He takes us through a process to strip away our carnal lusts. In my life, my type was my father. When he metaphorically walked out my life through betrayal of trust, this created a dent within my soul. Subconsciously, all the boys following him reminded me of my father. Every time, I was attracted to the same kind of demon in a different kind of flesh.

2). *Lust of the Eyes*

Eve was deceived.

> **Genesis 3:6:** And when the woman saw that the tree was good for food, and that it was pleasant to the eyes, and a tree to be desired to make one wise, she took of the fruit thereof, and did eat, and gave also unto her husband with her; and he did eat (KJV).

Lust of the Flesh, Lust of the Eyes, and the Pride of Life

The tree of the knowledge of good and evil was pleasing to Eve's eyes. Beauty in itself is not sin. The Bible talks about beauty. David had attractive eyes and a handsome appearance. Joseph was so handsome that a married woman tried to sleep with him. Daniel was handsome and without blemish. Beauty can become a social construct that limits us to reject people outside of what we deem as attractive. This social construct is often based on our own voids. If we desire someone to be highly physically attractive to us, this means that we perhaps need to grow up a bit more until we value internal qualities rather than external qualities. This is my case, and that's okay. I do believe I will be physically attracted to my husband. I'm sure he will be pleasant to my eyes, but perhaps this might just be on a mild spectrum.

In my observation, I found that young women who have been sexually traumatized tend to care more about physical appearance in a potential mate than the average young woman. This is because they have been overly sexualized at a young age. There are five senses, which include sight, smell, hearing, taste, and touch. When you have been abused

Lust of the Flesh, Lust of the Eyes, and the Pride of Life

all your life, you naturally desire and seek out pleasure and pleasurable experiences. Pleasure and comfort can easily become an abuse survivor's God or idol. This often translates to how we pick and choose a mate. We want people to appeal to us in the natural, rather than the spiritual. This is because we believe the lie that the natural gives us the greatest pleasure and joy. The Bible says it otherwise.

> **Matthew 6:33:** But seek first his kingdom and his righteousness, and all these things will be given to you as well (NIV).

I want to clarify. I don't believe God will give you a husband that you find repulsive. The word repulsive means "arousing intense distaste or disgust" (Oxford Languages). It is hard to procreate and respect a man if you are too busy gagging at the sight of his appearance.

A lie that single young women believe is that marriage is all about sex. That lie comes from the pit of hell. Marriage is spent standing up or sleeping. According to a married woman, every sexual encounter in a marriage is twenty to thirty minutes. If you learn your husband, you will shorten this time. Your husband won't want to have sex every night. At max, you will have sex three to four times a week. This will lessen when you get older.

> In a study of over 26,000 Americans, which was published in the Archives of Sexual Behavior, participants reported having sex 54 times a year, which averages out to approximately once a week (Reference: Psychology Today, How Often Should Couples Have Sex?)

Some young women believe that, as helpmeets, all they need to master is being good in the bedroom and learning to cook and clean. You are more than a sex object and a housemaid. Marriage is more than sex and having a clean home.

Sometimes, when young women have not had a solid father figure in their lives, they end up dating pedophiles. A pedophile is an older man who prefers a woman who speaks, acts, and dresses like a child. This woman tends to be one to two decades younger than him. He wants to exert toxic power and dominance over her. As a result, he treats her like a child. He doesn't see himself as her partner in crime, rather he sees her as a slave. These relationships end up pretty abusive, so if you haven't dealt with your father wounds, you aren't ready for a relationship, let alone marriage. Women, in these types of marriages often find themselves outgrowing their voids, and they almost always end up leaving the abusive marriages.

Oxford Languages define pleasure as, "a feeling of happy satisfaction and enjoyment." You will feel more enjoyment married to a man who loves you, rather than a man who is simply after your body. There's joy in shopping in a market, reading in a coffee shop, or climbing the mountains together. These activities bring pleasure to the eyes, nose, and ears. Eating a good meal together brings out the pleasure of taste. Having a hug brings out oxytocin similar to eating a good chocolate bar. Some women don't feel pleasure in having sex, and sex for them, is actually quite painful. To marry someone based on wanting a good time in the bedroom will prove to be a generational curse in the making. My point is, it is better to marry someone you actually enjoy being around, rather than a good sex partner.

3). Pride of Life

The pride of life is essentially the desire to gain the approval of a certain group of people. These people whom we desire approval from are often the ones who have rejected us or made us feel rejected in the past. These can also be people who we admire or look up to. It is dangerous to elevate anyone above God. Proverbs 29:25 reads, "Fear of man will prove to be a snare, but whoever trusts in the Lord is kept safe" (NIV). The synonym for the word snare is trap. Essentially, when we fear man, we are setting the stage for our own demise by walking ourselves into a man-made trap. Ultimately, the decision to fear God's opinion above man's opinion lies within our own hands. Jeremiah 17:5 reads, "This is what the Lord says: 'Cursed is the one who trusts in man, who draws strength from mere flesh and whose heart turns away from the Lord'" (NIV). This verse implies that trusting in man or man's opinion is putting value or confidence in our flesh, thereby, allowing our hearts to reject God.

Lust of the Flesh, Lust of the Eyes, and the Pride of Life

    In terms of desiring an attractive spouse, young women have a tendency to want to date based on the opinions of their peers and families' expectations for them. It's because their 'desire' will be for their husband. This actually indicates a form of possession. That is why there is a tendency for young women to idolize (possess) the opposite gender. Some young women tend to be jealous and competitive in nature. This manifests in using men as objects. Women can easily turn men into objects and use them as trophies to measure their success in society. Usually, when women get into relationships, their friends' immediate responses are, "Can I see a picture? What does he look like?" Other questions their friends may ask include, "What kind job does he have? Does he have a house?" If their peers and family members deem him to be attractive or rich, this adds a confidence boost to the woman. Unfortunately, these young women are still subject to the culture's opinion of them. If I am honest, this is something I still need to wrestle down.

    If we fear someone else's potential rejection, we have elevated that person's opinion above God's opinion. Therefore, we need to repent of idolatry. Idolatry does not please God. In fact, it infuriates Him. Our Father in Heaven is similar to a husband who becomes jealous when his wife flirts with other men. The husband has a right to be jealous when his wife flirts with other men because of the covenant that was established between the two of them. Like the husband, God, the Creator of the universe, has every right to long for His creation to worship, praise, honor, and adore Him. When the wife's affections are stirred towards other men, she is essentially rejecting her husband's love and neglecting to remember her husband's faithfulness towards her. Naturally, this would upset her husband who has sacrificed immensely for his wife.

The following verses describe this matter in detail:

> **Exodus 20:5:** You shall not bow down to them or serve them, for I the Lord your God am a jealous God, visiting the iniquity of the fathers on the children to the third and the fourth generation of those who hate me (ESV).

Exodus 34:14: (for you shall worship no other god, for the Lord, whose name is Jealous, is a jealous God) (ESV).

Deuteronomy 4:24: For the Lord your God is a consuming fire, a jealous God (ESV).

2 Corinthians 11:2: For I feel a divine jealousy for you, since I betrothed you to one husband, to present you as a pure virgin to Christ (ESV).

Deuteronomy 6:15: For the Lord your God in your midst is a jealous God—lest the anger of the Lord your God be kindled against you, and he destroy you from off the face of the earth (ESV).

Isaiah 42:8: I am the Lord; that is my name; my glory I give to no other, nor my praise to carved idols (ESV).

Deuteronomy 32:16: They stirred him to jealousy with strange gods; with abominations they provoked him to anger (ESV).

Chapter 10

The Product of Trauma is an Adulterous Woman

The Israelites were unable to be steadfastly loyal to God. Ezekiel 16 compares the Israelites to an adulterous wife. **Isaiah 54:5:** For your Maker is your husband, the LORD of hosts is his name; and the Holy One of Israel is your Redeemer, the God of the whole earth he is called. In the Bible, God is represented as our husband (ESV).

> **Ezekiel 16:4-5:** On the day you were born your cord was not cut, nor were you washed with water to make you clean, nor were you rubbed with salt or wrapped in cloths. No one looked on you with pity or had compassion enough to do any of these things for you. Rather, you were thrown out into the

open field, for on the day you were born you were despised (NIV).

This describes the adulterous wife as an infant. She comes from an abusive background. No one cared to even cut her umbilical cord. She was unwashed and unkempt. This shows that she was unwanted. The infant was even thrown into an open field. She was despised. Childhood abuse survivors can relate to this kind of reality. We were metaphorically thrown out into the open field and left to take care of ourselves.

Ezekiel 16:6-8: Then I passed by and saw you kicking about in your blood, and as you lay there in your blood I said to you, "Live!" I made you grow like a plant of the field. You grew and developed and entered puberty. Your breasts had formed and your hair had grown, yet you were stark naked. Later I passed by, and when I looked at you and saw that you were old enough for love, I spread the corner of my garment over you and covered your naked body. I gave you my solemn oath and entered into a covenant with you,

The Product of Trauma is an Adulterous Woman

declares the Sovereign Lord, and you became mine (NIV).

This describes her husband, God. He met Jerusalem at her weakest moment. She was on the floor bleeding. She begins to grow into a young woman. God saw that she was naked and He clothed her. He enters into a covenant (an agreement) with her. For a trauma survivor, this is when God encounters her and gives her a new life.

> **Ezekiel 16:9-14:** I bathed you with water and washed the blood from you and put ointments on you. I clothed you with an embroidered dress and put sandals of fine leather on you. I dressed you in fine linen and covered you with costly garments. I adorned you with jewelry: I put bracelets on your arms and a necklace around your neck, and I put a ring on your nose, earrings on your ears and a beautiful crown on your head. So you were adorned with gold and silver; your clothes were of fine linen and costly fabric and embroidered cloth. Your food was honey, olive oil and the finest flour. <u>You became very</u>

<u>beautiful and rose to be a queen.</u> And your fame spread among the nations on account of your beauty, because the splendor I had given you made your beauty perfect, declares the Sovereign Lord (NIV).

God, the husband of the adulterous woman, takes care of her by bathing her and putting expensive ointments, clothing, and jewelry on her. God takes her reproach away from her abandonment and helps her rise up to become a queen. This woman becomes famous because of God.

Ezekiel 16:15-22: But you trusted in your beauty and used your fame to become a prostitute. You lavished your favors on anyone who passed by and your beauty became his. You took some of your garments to make gaudy high places, where you carried on your prostitution. You went to him, and he possessed your beauty. <u>You also took the fine jewelry I gave you, the jewelry made of my gold and silver, and you made for yourself male idols and engaged in prostitution with them</u>. And

you took your embroidered clothes to put on them, and you offered my oil and incense before them. Also the food I provided for you—the flour, olive oil and honey I gave you to eat—you offered as fragrant incense before them. That is what happened, declares the Sovereign LORD.
And you took your sons and daughters whom you bore to me and sacrificed them as food to the idols. Was your prostitution not enough? You slaughtered my children and sacrificed them to the idols. In all your detestable practices and your prostitution, you did not remember the days of your youth, when you were naked and bare, kicking about in your blood (NIV).

Unfortunately, Jerusalem does not remember that her favor and good gifts came from her God, not her beauty and fame. She failed to recognize where all the blessings came from. The prostitute shrines were designed to worship false deities through orgies. Jerusalem begins to worship other gods. She has many idols. She does not remember her youth when she was broken,

The Product of Trauma is an Adulterous Woman

bruised, and battered. Due to their unresolved trauma, trauma survivors are often in severe emotional pain. They turn to other sources to numb the pain. Those sources are often band-aids. Many trauma survivors use men as miniature idols in whom they bow down to and give their bodies or hearts to, so they can gain a morsel of affection. This high doesn't last but for a moment. Unfortunately, as time passes, addiction also enters the picture. For me, I became addicted to the euphoria I felt when I liked a boy, even if it wasn't true love. This became my drug of choice whenever I was going through a hard time. Left to our own devices, we continue on this destructive path until God intervenes.

> **Ezekiel 16:23-31:** Woe! Woe to you, declares the Sovereign LORD. In addition to all your other wickedness, you built a mound for yourself and made a lofty shrine in every public square. At every street corner, you built your lofty shrines and degraded your beauty, spreading your legs with increasing promiscuity to anyone who passed by. You engaged in prostitution with the Egyptians, your neighbors with large genitals, and

aroused my anger with your increasing promiscuity. So I stretched out my hand against you and reduced your territory; I gave you over to the greed of your enemies, the daughters of the Philistines, who were shocked by your lewd conduct. You engaged in prostitution with the Assyrians too, because you were insatiable; and even after that, you still were not satisfied. Then you increased your promiscuity to include Babylonia, a land of merchants, but even with this you were not satisfied. I am filled with fury against you, declares the Sovereign LORD, when you do all these things, acting like a brazen prostitute! When you built your mounds at every street corner and made your lofty shrines in every public square, you were unlike a prostitute, because you scorned payment (NIV).

Jerusalem lives a promiscuous lifestyle. She wants the attention from other men, even from the Egyptians who had their own set of idols. Jerusalem has unquenchable and insatiable lusts, so she believes that these men from different ethnicities will satisfy her hunger.

The Product of Trauma is an Adulterous Woman

She has forgotten her humble upbringing, and the God who brought her out of her misery. Although, she still has access to God and His resources, she acts like a shrine prostitute. Even after a trauma survivor becomes a believer, if she continues to run from her past, she will subconsciously run after other idols in an attempt to ease her suffering.

> **Ezekiel 16:32-42:** You adulterous wife! You prefer strangers to your own husband! All prostitutes receive gifts, but you give gifts to all your lovers, bribing them to come to you from everywhere for your illicit favors. So in your prostitution you are the opposite of others; no one runs after you for your favors. You are the very opposite, for you give payment and none is given to you. " 'Therefore, you prostitute, hear the word of the Lord! This is what the Sovereign Lord says: Because you poured out your lust and exposed your naked body in your promiscuity with your lovers, and because of all your detestable idols, and because you gave them your children's blood, therefore I am going to gather all your lovers, with

whom you found pleasure, those you loved as well as those you hated. I will gather them against you from all around and will strip you in front of them, and they will see you stark naked. I will sentence you to the punishment of women who commit adultery and who shed blood; I will bring on you the blood vengeance of my wrath and jealous anger. Then I will deliver you into the hands of your lovers, and they will tear down your mounds and destroy your lofty shrines. They will strip you of your clothes and take your fine jewelry and leave you stark naked. They will bring a mob against you, who will stone you and hack you to pieces with their swords. They will burn down your houses and inflict punishment on you in the sight of many women. I will put a stop to your prostitution, and you will no longer pay your lovers. Then my wrath against you will subside and my jealous anger will turn away from you; I will be calm and no longer angry (NIV).

God rebukes her. There are consequences for her actions. A loving God disciplines His children. Jerusalem faces the consequences for her disobedience. God chooses to allow Jerusalem to suffer from her idolatry of sex and romantic love. The men she'd worshiped left her empty and dry. The houses where she acted as a harlot will be burned down. God wants her prostitution and lewd acts to cease. God is a jealous husband. He doesn't want us to worship other gods. As a trauma survivor, it is easy to go through cycles and cycles of men. This addiction doesn't seem to cease. We try our methods, but nothing seems to work. Every time, we are triggered, we subconsciously run to romantic love or sex. This is when God intervenes. He often has to bring us to a painful place. He allows us to witness the depravity of our idolatry. Our idols fail us, and we are left in severe pain. We are forced to face the reality that the very idols that we had hoped to bring us healing from our rejection and abandonment are the very things that deepen the voids within our souls.

> **Ezekiel 16:59-63:** This is what the Sovereign LORD says: I will deal with you as you deserve, because you have despised my oath by breaking the

covenant. Yet I will remember the covenant I made with you in the days of your youth, and I will establish an everlasting covenant with you. Then you will remember your ways and be ashamed when you receive your sisters, both those who are older than you and those who are younger. I will give them to you as daughters, but not on the basis of my covenant with you. <u>So I will establish my covenant with you, and you will know that I am the Lord. Then, when I make atonement for you for all you have done, you will remember and be ashamed and never again open your mouth because of your humiliation, declares the Sovereign Lord (NIV).</u>

In the end, Jerusalem, the unfaithful, adulterous wife breaks the covenant she has with God. God remembers the agreement that He has made with her in her youth. God keeps His promises, because He is unable to lie. God makes reparation for a wrong or injury committed by Jerusalem herself. She will remember that the Lord is her husband. She will recognize the grace undeserved. He once again takes away the reproach from the lewd acts of her adult years, just as He takes away the reproach she felt when her parents abandoned her. For a trauma survivor, God will strip us away from our idols. It feels like we are dying, because we believe that these idols will bring us everlasting joy. In fact, these idols are slowly killing us. God will take away the shame from our previous mishaps. Whatever sexual sin we committed (fantasy, romantic soul-ties, fornication), God will cover our shame when we turn our hearts back to Him. God knows that the path you walked hasn't been easy. He has great compassion and mercy on you. He was singing over you when you were in your mother's womb, even if you were an unwanted pregnancy.

Chapter 11

Unrequited Love and the Samaritan Woman

As a young woman, unrequited love is a personal death, especially if we have never had true love from our families of origin. As a grown woman, we can look back and laugh at ourselves. We laugh because we were so young and immature that we had mistaken obsession for love, lust for love, and strong affection for love. If we are honest with ourselves though, we remember the pain and the anguish we felt because we thought that love had died. I've experienced the anguish of fresh heartbreak, and I responded by crying into my pillow and chopping my long locks into a short bob.

Before I share my personal story, I will share a story of Corrie Ten Boom, a Dutch Christian watchmaker, who helped many Jews escape from the Nazis during the Holocaust by hiding them in her home. Corrie Ten Boom was an inspirational woman of God, yet, she never got married. This doesn't exempt the fact that she is human and that God designed women differently than men.

> **Genesis 3:16:** To the woman he said, "I will make your pains in childbearing very severe; with painful labor you will give birth to children. <u>Your desire will be for your husband,</u> and he will rule over you" (NIV).

The word desire is Hebrew for *teshuwqah,* which means:
- desire
- longing
- craving

Oxford Languages define desire as "a strong feeling of wanting to have something or wishing for something to happen." Essentially, a woman will have a strong feeling or longing for a husband.

I believe the reason why the desire for men is placed in every woman is so that procreation will occur on this Earth. Women, in every way, are as capable, perhaps, even more capable than men at living successful, happy, and whole lives. Remember, Adam needed help, not Eve. Women are receptors. Men are imparters. The only need a grown woman has for a grown man is for his impartation, so children will come forth. Other than that, a grown woman in this day and age can live a flourishing and abundant life without a grown man as her husband. The desire for a husband isn't an evil one. It's a God-given desire. For the young woman who has yet to know her true value or worth, this desire often becomes uncontrollable and unquenchable. This is when the desire becomes an idol. Once, the young woman encounters the Lord as her husband, the desire for a husband ceases until it becomes *almost* non-existent, as she is too busy doing God's business to obsess over what she does not have. Sometimes, it would appear that she has the gift of celibacy. This is not the case; it's just that she becomes infatuated with God, her husband.

Sometimes, young women wonder why men can easily get over them, while women are left crying many months or years thereafter. The curse of the woman is to long for the man. When a man imparts a bit of strength or 'supposed strength' inside of her, she is left barren when he walks away. She, in turn, becomes a mad woman, desperately seeking for another impartation of the strength that was given to her. This, in turn, creates a desperate longing to run after another man, even if she hasn't fully processed the last man who left her.

That's why fathers are so important in the life of a young woman. They act as a guard to filter the trash from the treasure. Young woman, honor the spiritual fathers God has placed in your life.

In Corrie Ten Boom's story, she first meets a young man named Karel, her older brother, Willem's friend at her mother's get together. He is very kind to her, and he is also handsome. As a teenager, Corrie Ten Boom is insecure about her appearance. She also doesn't get much attention from the boys at her school. She often admires the composure and poise of her older sister, while she is shy and has plain looks. Whenever Karel came to visit her older brother, Karel also used this as an opportunity to talk with Corrie. Corrie and Karel would take long strolls and share their hopes and dreams together. When Karel was away, he and her would write corresponding letters to each other. Corrie's older brother warned her that Karel would never be able to marry her because he was from a wealthy, prominent family. Corrie, being a teenager, didn't guard her heart. One day, Karel came to visit their family with his fiancé on his arm. Corrie was heartbroken, because she believed that there was a possibility that he would propose to her. Nevertheless, she held her composure with the help of her entire family until Karel and his fiancé left. After that, she ran up to her room and cried. Corrie wrote the following:

> "How long I lay on my bed sobbing for the one love of my life I do not know. I was afraid of what father would say. Afraid he would say, "There'll be someone else soon," and that forever afterwards this untruth would lie between us. "Corrie," he began instead, "do you know what hurts so very much? It's love. Love is the strongest force in the world, and when it is blocked that means pain. There are two things we

can do when this happens. We can kill the love so that it stops hurting. But then of course part of us dies, too. Or, Corrie, we can ask God to open up another route for that love to travel. God loves Karel, even more than you do, and if you ask Him, He will give you His love for this man, a love nothing can prevent, nothing destroy. Whenever we cannot love in the old human way, God can give us the perfect way."

"I did not know that he had put into my hands the secret that would open far darker rooms than this; places where there was not, on a human level, anything to love at all. My task just then was to give up my feeling for Karel without giving up the joy and wonder that had grown with it. And so, that very hour, I whispered a prayer, "Lord, I give to You the way I feel about Karel, my thoughts about our future, everything! Give me Your way of seeing Karel instead. Help me to love him that way. That much" (Reference: The Hiding Place: The Triumphant True Story of Corrie Ten Boom, Corrie Ten Boom).

Unrequited Love and the Samaritan Woman

I too had my fair share of unrequited love instances, as I was always the girl chasing the boys.

Disclaimer: This is an excerpt from my journal. It was written during the time I was still grieving the losses. The emotions are raw, vulnerable, and unprocessed. I edited the entry for grammatical errors. I offer this to you as a guide to help process your losses in your unrequited love. I went through the seven stages of grief (shock, denial, anger, bargaining, depression, testing, and acceptance) with this one boy. I obsessed over him, hated him, wished he would die, wished I could see him, and eventually all the feelings I had for him died. I still care about him as a sister in Christ, and I pray that he marries a woman much better than me. I pray that he accomplishes all that God has for him. In this raw post, you can see how I idealized him because of my own childhood trauma. If I had a strong relationship with God back then and if I would've known who I was, I wouldn't have ever liked him. I picked him because of my voids and insecurities. I didn't stay long enough to see his demons manifest, so it was easy for me to idealize him. God protected me from him. We had two different callings in our lives.

Undated Journal Entry

The other day, I finally garnered the courage to finally rip the note off of my birthday card from the boy I had secretly pined over since my sophomore year in college. The note consisted of an apology from him for judging me, because I wrote such a preposterous song about sacrificing him in a pit of fire. He wrote to me that my heart for God was beautiful. I was young, immature and emotionally stunted.

I met him during a sophomore and freshmen gathering at my church. The first time I met him, perhaps I did find him attractive. Yet, my defense mechanism pushed me to internally and proudly declare, "I like White boys, not Korean boys!"

To be fair, as a new Christian, the church indoctrinated us so that we would regard the opposite gender as brothers or sisters. He's your b-r-o-t-h-e-r. There seemed to be no room for shenanigans. The idea of liking my brother grossed me out like no other, so I declared him to be off-limits. Despite that fact, I still wanted him close to me.

At the gathering, he played guitar beautifully and sung well, too. I was enamored and awestruck. A friendly sense of admiration began to well up from the bottom of my heart.

As I observed him on Sundays, I noted that I would want to be with someone of that sort one day, passionately in love with God, raising his hands, and occasionally spurting into tongues. The church I attended in high school heavily believed in the gifts of the Holy Spirit such as healing, miracles, prophecy, and tongues. I believed the lie that the gift of tongues was a super gift that only special people were given. How immature I was! The sense of admiration grew in my heart. To me, he wasn't an ordinary boy, but a special boy.

After the gathering, I was the first to initiate a conversation with him and I boldly added him on Facebook, sending him a message stating that I wanted to be a very good friend of his. Oh, how I regret messaging him now; it would have never led to such deep heartbreak.

The problem with the idealization or admiration of any human being is that it leads to disillusionment. The person you see on the outside is only a fragment of who they really are. This is why dating is not just a fun game where frills, jewels, and chocolates are exchanged. It's an evaluation and interview process to pick the best candidate for marriage, a life-long covenant. It's also a very dangerous process. One overly invested soul can lead to premature devastation.

I would also like to note at this point that this boy and I never dated. It was a situationship, a simple one-sided admiration on my part.

As I began to talk to him online, I didn't realize how quickly I was becoming attached to him. Fear rose in my heart. This began a confusing array of communication on my end. I started to vulnerably, casually, and without much thought, disclose details of my day and my own feelings regarding certain events in my life. Yet, in person, I would ignore him and disdain his existence. To be truthful, I was afraid of rejection, but I also wanted to be close. This was the only way for me to handle my heart safely, or so I thought at the time.

As I disclosed more about myself through messenger, I let down layers of myself. These were my deepest thoughts that I would only disclose to my closest female friends. How I wish I could turn back the hands of time and tell the younger me to guard my heart!

In the meanwhile, I also had one-on-ones with other boys. I grew close enough to them, but I also kept them far away enough where I felt safe. I was deathly afraid that commitment meant the loss of control and the possibility of disappointment.

Eventually, God called him overseas to the heart of his motherland. I was actually extremely bitter and angry with God when I heard the news that he was going to leave. This person unfortunately became an idol in my heart. When he left, I felt abandoned. To be direct, at that time, I was a baby believer. I wasn't even able to recognize what an idol was. I believed uncontrollably crushing on a chain of boys was a normal occurrence for any young girl!

He left for his motherland and I cried. My obsession with him grew to such a strong infatuation that a soul-tie began to form. Satan used my own spirit of rejection and my own dreams against me. Eventually, I believed an outrageous lie that this boy was my future husband.

It didn't help that he had a heart for the very country that I would come to live and serve in.

Throughout his time in his motherland, I held on tightly to him. I was praying to God that he would provide a way for us to have a favorable outcome when he arrived back to the States. My hope slowly turned from my God, my Savior, to this boy.

Two years later, he returned to the States. The first gathering at my church for my servants' team took place, and I couldn't even look him in the eyes. My own obsession with him dehumanized him into an object, and I immediately noticed his outward flaws. "He's a lot shorter than I remembered him." This was a passing thought of mine.

To be fair, my automatic reaction to his physical appearance was my internal defense mechanism coming out. This defense mechanism was my self-constructed protective barrier designed to help me defend myself from any self-perceived dangers. His height never bothered me in the past.

I also discovered that his hometown changed his character for the worst. He wasn't the guy I remembered or admired. He cared too much about his physical appearance. He was loud to a fault, and sometimes, he overtly disagreed with authority. Admittedly, he was a lot cuter because he'd gotten a perm. Truthfully, the deeper substance and character I mistakenly saw when I first met him was just an illusion to present reality.

Perhaps, I didn't even really know him at all in the first place. By this stage, I was already too emotionally invested in my idea to even think of giving up on him. I wrestled with God. I used his physical appearance as an excuse to negate the internal red flags I saw visibly in him.

I desperately wanted God to give me the desire of my heart. I wanted God to allow a relationship with this boy to foster. For me, I was already in too deep. I didn't want to face the truth that I'd wasted an exuberant amount of time and emotional resources liking an unhealthy person.

Little did I know at the time, he was already in a long-distance relationship with his girlfriend, a woman who he'd met in his motherland.

For an entire year, I prayed for courage. I prayed for God to open doors for our friendship to develop. I prayed that God would allow me to see him as a brother. As God opened these doors, I naively allowed these individual answered prayers to become signs leading to a bigger confirmation that we were meant to be.

One little door that God opened was during the end of the semester. He forgot his wallet at church, and I decided to treat him to a meal. Looking back now, it wasn't out of a pure heart to love him as a sister. It was more of a desperate plea. "Pick me! I'm nice! Pick me! I'll treat you well! "Why won't you pick me?"

My friends saw the red flags in him. My guy friend, who was his Bible study leader, told me that he was very prideful. He wouldn't even listen to his instructions, but would argue instead. My girlfriend told me that she saw lust in his eyes.

I stubbornly didn't listen with completely open ears. After all, I still held on to the lie that because "God" gave me a dream about him, he had to be my husband. Lies. It was Satan, but I didn't see it at the time.

Long story short, my fantasy world of us doing ministry together began to take a huge toll on my life. I envisioned what married life with this person would be like. These fantasies became more and more engrossed and obsessive.

As I was serving God by co-leading a small group of women, this idol in my heart began to grow into my hope for my own future. It began to take away my joy in God. I spent the majority of my time praying about the situation with the boy, pleading with God to allow us to become an item, if it was in His will.

In the end, God said no.

In the post listed above, I was in the wrong. It was my fault for allowing this boy to have access to me.

I pursued a relationship with a boy. I initiated a relationship by asking to become his close friend. I initiated the relationship by pursuing him on messenger. He clearly was not interested in me. He was interested in my interest and my desperate pursuit. If he truly wanted to be with me, he would've asked me to be his girlfriend. I didn't guard my heart by revealing my deepest fears, dreams, insecurities, and hopes. Those topics should be kept close to your own heart and shared with certain people of your own gender. I mistook giftedness for character. I didn't look for good internal fruits, but just outward manifestations of the Holy Spirit. I ignored the red flags. I ignored the truth that my friends saw in him. I ignored the fact that he was prideful, lustful, and angry. I viewed myself as the pursuer and not the prize. Women are NOT supposed to pursue men for a good reason. I had insecurity, abandonment, and rejection issues that stemmed from my childhood. This boy was a band-aid and distraction from the real pain that was going on inside. I was NOT ready to even consider being in a relationship. I saw potential instead of accepting the reality of who he was. Many people have potential. Few reach their potential. I spent too much time meditating on him, rather than Christ. I entertained fantasy. I assumed that this boy was my husband without testing the spirits behind the dream I was given. I got ahead of myself, and I dreamed of a future into existence. The future that I dreamt of with him stemmed from my voids. I didn't allow God to fill my voids. I wasn't baptized and filled with the Holy Ghost. I turned to him for my comfort and encouragement, instead of God. I didn't know who I was, so I was looking to find myself in and through him. I mistook pity and compassion for love. I later learned about his difficult upbringing, and I couldn't stop crying for him. Later, I learned that it had triggered something within me. I was crying for myself and the childhood I lost. I had undelivered spirits inside of me, so my demons were attracted to his demons. I was not whole and healed, so I also attracted a broken soul.

    The best revenge you can give to a person who has hurt you in a previous situationship or relationship is to forgive that person, move on, and grow up. Become everything God put on the inside of you and actualize it.

Once again, if I was whole and delivered, had a genuine relationship with the Holy Spirit, I would've never gotten myself in such a painful predicament. When God called me to East Asia, little did I know at the time, God was propelling me into a season of healing and service. As I shared the gospel, ministered to the girls on campus, God was healing me as I was healing them. The irony of it all was the girls that I met on campus the first semester all had unresolved soul-ties. My stories encouraged them to process their pain and quickly move on.

God refreshes those who refresh others.

God also sent me a spiritual family. This family showed me healthy storge. I was able to experience a Christmas like no other when I first came to East Asia. We all watched a movie called Coco's together. In my family of origin, I spent the majority of my Christmases alone. I felt God's love through their love. Despite the fact that I don't like to celebrate my birthdays, my spiritual family made the effort to make it special every year. My first year on the field, Bethany got me a huge bear. She told me that I didn't need to wait for a man to get me a huge stuffed animal, because she would do so for me. She also told me that her own father never got her a huge stuffed bear, and I was absolutely touched. The older brother on the field taught us how to cook. Bethany and I would come every Friday to cook together with the help of the missionary brother.

The missionary family treated me like I was their own daughter. That was very healing for me. The missionary father was a humorous man. He liked to make vlogs and learn different languages. We had that in common. The missionary mother was talented in baking, and she personally mentored me for two years.

These relationships were definitely not perfect, yet the love within those relationships was genuine. Due to my own dysfunction, I had to do a lot of forgiving and reconciling, but God was in the center of it all. Ironically, during the healing process, I desperately hungered for eros, however, God wanted to show me agape, storge, and phileo. Eros was my drug of choice, and I felt like a famished animal without food. Every time I saw an attractive member of the opposite gender, I yearned to pursue him, as I had done in the past. Although I did make some mistakes during my time of healing, God was still faithful to me. As I was healing from my soul tie, I was like the Samaritan woman. Although I had my five 'husbands,' I still proudly declared to the young women on campus that Jesus is Lord.

    The Samaritan woman was a woman who had five husbands and the sixth man she was living with wasn't really her husband. The reason she had all these men was because she had an unquenchable thirst deep inside of her soul. We don't know much about her background or why she became this woman who needed men so much. Yet, I know that we all can empathize with her. We understand that longing inside of her soul to be held, loved, touched, and affirmed. Yet, when she encounters Jesus by the well, Jesus gives her a word of knowledge that forever shapes her destiny. He sees her for who she has become, but doesn't let her stay there. He offers her life that goes beyond the life she could see in front of her eyes. He offers a river of flowing water.

He offers her a kind of water (lifestyle) that will quench her thirst forever. That living water struck her in such a profound way that she left her bucket and ran back to her town to tell everyone about the prophet who is her Messiah. Jesus Christ is the Messiah that her people had been waiting for. The most special part is that He'd picked her out of everyone in the town of Samaria to first reveal Himself to. He used her to be the avenue for other people's salvation. After that, I believe her life was changed, and she decided to spend her life telling everyone about the Messiah.

How many 'husbands' have you had? What kind of condition (emotionally, mentally, physically, financially) were you in when you got with them? If you know what you know now, would have you picked them?

Chapter 12

The Power of Esther and Ruth, God's Ordained Spouse for You

Did you know Esther was an orphan? Before she arose to become queen, she was raised by her cousin, Mordecai. There was a huge risk when she entered the pageant, because she could have potentially become a concubine. A concubine is similar to a woman on the welfare system who is forever dependent on the government to provide for her basic needs. The king gave them housing, food, and basic necessities in exchange for their bodies. Once the king slept with the women, he forgot most of their names. Most concubines were unable to become pregnant because the king only slept with them once before tossing them aside. In biblical days, the queen was the king's main woman.

The Power of Esther and Ruth, God's Ordained Spouse for You

When Queen Vashti dishonored the pagan king, she lost her position as queen. In turn, King Xerxes held a beauty pageant for women of the neighboring region to determine who the next queen would be. Imagine how hard it was for little Esther, who was just 14-years old at the time. The other women probably grew up in lavish environments, had luxurious purple robes, and ate the most expensive delicacies, while Esther grew up feeling a deep sense of humiliation regarding who she was. She didn't grow up with a silver spoon in her mouth. Fortunately, Esther had an advantage over the other women. Esther didn't rely on her beauty or her brains. Her previous traumas in life humbled her, and she was able to see herself in a sober light. She knew of her value, yet she knew that she couldn't rely on just her abilities or physicality. She relied on wisdom, revelation, and knowledge from the people she submitted to. That's why she won God's favor and became queen. Esther was also humble enough to remember her upbringing. She chose to risk her life to save her people, the Jews. God's favor was on her, thus the king granted her request. She became her peoples' deliverer. *What God delivers you* from is what you are called to deliver others from!

> **Galatians 4:1-7:** What I am saying is that as long as an heir is underage, he is no different from a slave, although he owns the whole estate. <u>The heir is subject to guardians and trustees **until the time** set by his father</u>. So also, when we were underage, we were in slavery under the elemental spiritual forces of the world. **But when the set time** <u>had fully come</u>, God sent his Son, born of a woman, born under the law, to redeem those under the law, that **<u>we might receive adoption to sonship</u>**. Because you are his sons, God sent the Spirit of his Son into our hearts, the Spirit who calls out, *"Abba,* Father." So you are no longer a slave, but God's child; and since you are his child, God has made you also an heir (NIV).

When we ask God for a husband or a blessing, this blessing is found in a person. If we are connected to the person in the proper way, we can receive the blessing. When we submit to another person, we are essentially receiving the mandate found on the other person's life. Honor bestows honor.

In the story of Ruth, Ruth left her people, the Moabites, after her husband passed away. She chose to forsake her own gods to follow the God of her mother-in-law, Naomi. Despite the fact that Naomi would not be able to provide a husband for her, Ruth is loyal to the authority above her. She submits to Naomi. This isn't a story about a woman pursuing a man. It's a story about honor and submission. Ruth wanted to be of help to Naomi. As it turned out, she happened to be on Boaz's field to pick grain.

> **Ruth 3:1-6:** One day Ruth's mother-in-law Naomi said to her, "My daughter, I must find a home for you, where you will be well provided for. Now Boaz, with whose women you have worked, is a relative of ours. Tonight he will be winnowing barley on the threshing floor. Wash, put on perfume, and get dressed in your best clothes. Then go down to the threshing floor, but don't let him

know you are there until he has finished eating and drinking. When he lies down, note the place where he is lying. Then go and uncover his feet and lie down. He will tell you what to do."
"I will do whatever you say," Ruth answered. So she went down to the threshing floor and did everything her mother-in-law told her to do (NIV).

Ruth honored her authority, Naomi, and she got her blessing. I would like to present a caveat here. We are honoring the position God has placed on the person, not the human being him/herself. Another caveat I would like to present is that if a mentor makes a suggestion that has no biblical standing or if you're confused by it, it is still <u>your</u> responsibility to take their words up in prayer and see if the Holy Spirit confirms the word. Our mentors and leaders are imperfect and can make mistakes. To the degree you fear submission is the degree you lack trust in God.

Proverbs 3:5-6: Trust in the LORD with all your heart and lean not on your own understanding; in all your ways **<u>submit</u>** to him, and he will make your paths straight (NIV). Submission is the act of yielding our own personal will for God's will. Our will usually is comprised of our wants, longings, and desires. Oxford Languages define will as "a deliberate or fixed desire or intention" or "the thing that one desires or ordains." In layman's terms, our will is our desire or our intention to obtain what we believe is best for us. In other translations of Proverbs 3:5-6, the word submit is substituted for the word acknowledge. The word acknowledge is Hebrew for *yada*, which means to know. When we are fearful towards God's intention or plan for our lives, we don't know God intimately and deeply enough. Therefore, we are unable to see God's goodness and love poured out to our lives. In all our ways, we must know (*yada*) him. If we don't know God as our protector, we will see every leader who gives us a suggestion that is contrary to our desires as a weapon formed against us. In fact, God's ways often go beyond our understanding and logic. After all, His ways are not our ways; His thoughts are not our thoughts. His ways are higher than our ways; His thoughts are higher than our thoughts (Isaiah 55:8-9). **Proverbs 14:12** puts it this way, "There is a way *that seems* right to a man, but its end *is* the way of death" (NKJV). In essence, we must step out in faith during our healing journey. What we believe is best for us isn't always what's best for us. Compared to God, our understanding and perspective towards life is limited. We must ask God to help us lean not our own understanding but on His understanding. During our healing journey, God may ask us to do a lot of things that we think are absolutely crazy. During these moments, we must step out in faith.

When our mentors or spiritual leaders give us a suggestion, it may contradict our wants, longings, and desires. When Jezebel has controlled us for the majority of our lives, every person in authority appears to be Jezebel in disguise. We, thereby, become overly suspicious of every person in authority. Essentially, they all look like demons trained to rape, molest, and/or abuse us. Truthfully, our discernment is broken. We must grow in our understanding of God's Word. That way, we may be able to truly discern between what is good and/or evil.

Any idea or suggestion that stretches us out of our comfort zones triggers the scared little girls inside of us. Therefore, we are tempted to run. Running away from our mentors is not the solution to dissipating the fear. This fear goes deeper. We must wrestle down the offense that we feel towards our leaders, because they triggered the fear of being controlled within us. Practically speaking, this fear is wrestled down within our prayer closets. We must honestly express to God our raw emotions and fears in regards to our leaders' suggestions. We must honestly express the unpleasant feelings we have towards our leaders to God. We must also cancel out the word curses that we spoke about our leaders to God, after we express our fears to God. When we calm down, then we can hear the Holy Spirit's still, small voice. This is when we can objectively determine whether or not our leaders' suggestions align to the will of God. Nine out of ten times, our leaders have good intentions. **Jeremiah 3:15:** Then I will give you shepherds after my own heart, who will lead you with knowledge and understanding (NIV). Abuse survivors often yearn for people who understand and acknowledge their pain and current state/frame of mind. They are looking for empathy rather than information. For a season, it is necessary to grieve. Yet, in order to truly heal and move past our trauma, the grieving eventually has to cease. God wants us to grow past our pain, so we can become healthy functioning women of God, not stay little girls forever. In turn, we must have shepherds, leaders, mentors, and friends who have God's heart for us. These leaders will challenge, rebuke, and correct us. Do I have fuzzy feelings after being rebuked by mentors? Um, no. Let me repeat, um no. Fortunately, rebuke is for the wise. Rebuke is actually a form of love.

> **Proverbs 9:8-9:** Do not reprove a scoffer, or he will hate you; reprove a wise man, and he will love you. Give instruction to a wise man, and he will be still wiser; teach a righteous man, and he will increase in learning (ESV).
>
> **Proverbs 27:5:** Better is open rebuke than hidden love (ESV).

Have you ever had a friend that talked badly about you behind your back, yet smiled in front of your face? Didn't you feel betrayed? That is what happens when we only want to listen to sweet words. Flattery and compliments are what your abusive exes poured in your ears. Did these words help you grow wiser, better, stronger, and more competent? Take some time to really reflect on this. Perhaps, you would find, these sweet words were actually manipulative tactics to get you to stay in a toxic relationship. God disciplines His children. A form of abusive and negligent parenting is called permissive parenting. This is when parents fail to provide structure or discipline to their children. Often, these children grow up to become narcissists. In fact, structure and discipline help us properly grow. I often see crooked trees in East Asia. When this happens, the gardeners have to put a stake in the tree. Poles surround the tree, and metal wire is used to pull the tree into a straight alignment. This appears to be a painful and damaging process. In reality, in the long term, this benefits the tree. The crooked tree has a second chance in life to grow straight. Now, isn't that real love? The journey to wholeness is indeed painful, because God is untwisting us from all the lies that we have believed.

What is a Shepard? A Shepard is responsible for bringing the sheep inside the gate and outside the gate to feed in the pasture. The Shepard's rod and staff reels the stubborn sheep from running off of the cliff. Unfortunately, when one sheep runs off the cliff or leaves a congregation for unbiblical reasons, this often creates division within the church. This blind sheep often leads other blind sheep. One blind sheep runs off the cliff, thereby, other blind sheep follow. When we prematurely leave a church because of fear, offense, or other unbiblical reasons, we not only divide the church, but we also shortstop our season of healing. The Israelites had to go around the same mountain over and over again. What should have taken the Israelites 11 days ended up costing them 40 precious years. If you want to meet your king, you must pass the tests that God has set before you. We can't do this by ourselves. Thanks to the Holy Spirit, the Word of God, our leaders, and our community, we aren't alone in our journey to wholeness.

> **Hebrews 13:17:** Have confidence in your leaders and submit to their authority, because they keep watch over you as those who must give an account. Do this so that their work will be a joy, not a burden, for that would be of no benefit to you (NIV).

In short, your leaders are held accountable to God. Nine out of ten times, your leaders are prayerful about the suggestions or ideas they tell you. If a leader really values their relationship with God, they will not randomly blurt out an idea that is irrelevant to God's call on your life. They won't dare lead God's flock astray. On the Day of Judgment, if they led you astray, they will have to pay a hefty price.

> **Jeremiah 23:1-4:** Woe to the shepherds who destroy and scatter the sheep of My pasture!" declares the LORD. Therefore this is what the LORD, the God of Israel, says about the shepherds who tend My people: "You have scattered My flock and driven them away, and have not attended to them.

Behold, I will attend to you for the evil of your deeds, declares the LORD.
Then I Myself will gather the remnant of My flock from all the lands to which I have banished them, and I will return them to their pasture, where they will be fruitful and multiply. I will raise up shepherds over them who will tend them, and they will no longer be afraid or dismayed, nor will any go missing, declares the LORD (BSB).

The lie the enemy wants to speak upon young women who have been abused is that people have the power to destroy you. People do not have any *true* power over you. People do NOT have the power to ruin your life. In fact, we have power over our pain. Our power lies in how we respond to the trauma that has been inflicted on us. We can respond in two ways. We can either seek healing to move forward or stay stuck in our pasts. This is our choice.

Pain cannot kill you. Demons and evil men do not have power over you. We have

God's authority over all wicked principalities and forces. In fact, what traumatized us only makes us stronger. I know at the moment, as you read this page, this may not be the case for you. Your trauma, abuse, rape, molestation, etc, may have left you crippled on the floor. You feel as if you are a dead horse being kicked over and over again. Yet, I promise you sister, this too shall pass! When you hit rock bottom, you can only move up. You will soon look back and see how all things work for the good of those who love Him and are called according to His purpose (Romans 8:28). Eventually, you will thank God for the pain, because the pain made you *even* more beautiful, strong, fervent, powerful, anointed, capable, and invincible. God will use your pain to complete a great call and purpose!

Psalm 56:3: When I am afraid, I put my trust in you (NIV).

Learn to take brave risks with God and people. When a woman starts a business, she often will encounter many toxic customers as well as many good customers. Unfortunately, there will be customers who want to manipulate her and bypass business protocol. If she encounters one bad business customer, there is a temptation to quit altogether. That isn't wise, since she is making more profits than losses. She must learn the loophole that allowed the malfunctioned order to occur or the toxic customer in. Thereby, she must learn to either tighten up her boundaries or create new systems.

      This is what a trauma survivor must do. With God's help, she must learn to take a leap of faith and invest her time, emotions, trust, resources, finances, and energy in the people God has placed in her life. Is that scary? Um, yes. If it wasn't scary, why would we need faith? Faith is the assurance of things hoped for, the conviction of things unseen (Hebrews 11:1). It wouldn't be faith if it wasn't scary. We must learn to do things and life afraid. This builds up our faith muscles. Just like running, it is unpleasant and rather painful at first. As we build up our lungs and legs, we grow to love the freedom and adrenaline we feel on the track.

When our leaders tell us to complete a task that challenges us, it is for our good.

> **Isaiah 54:2:** Enlarge the place of your tent, stretch your tent curtains wide, do not hold back; lengthen your cords, strengthen your stakes (NIV).

The purpose of a mentor and/or leader is to stretch, challenge, and grow you into your fullest potential. The mentor obeys God by pulling out what is inside of you. Imagine that your stomach is full of black goo. Inside the black goo are boxes of unwrapped gifts. Your mentor has to wear a kitchen glove to pull out the unwrapped gifts inside of you. Afterwards, your mentor helps you unwrap these gifts covered in black goo. This process is not fun for the both of you. The uncomfortable tasks given to you by your mentor can be seen as miniature tests given by God to you. If you have a problem with trusting God, you will have a problem trusting your mentor. Simply put, the mentor's role is to proclaim, admonish, teach you, with all wisdom so that she may present you fully mature in Christ (Colossians 1:28).

I will be transparent. Submission is one of my biggest areas of weakness. I believe submission is a form of trust. I still have major trust issues. (This shouldn't be an excuse for rebellion, though). Submission will always be a struggle for women due to the fall. After all, our desire is for our husbands. This includes the desire to control our husbands and exert our influence over what he has heard from God.

If we don't practice submission as single women, how will we be able to submit to our husbands in the future? (Again, I hear the sound of crickets.)

During the summer of my first year in East Asia, my mentor had suggested that I participate in our church's mission trips to two different countries. If I'm one hundred percent truthful, this was not *my* plan for *my* summer. During my time in these two countries, I had severe stomach issues. There were many physical discomforts, such as sleeping on the floor, eating strange delicacies, and standing in the hot sun for long hours. I had anticipated these discomforts in advance, so I wasn't looking forward to partaking in these trips.

When my mentor made the suggestion for me to go on these mission trips, the rebellious course of action would be to deceive her and say, "I'll be praying." Instead, I would appear to be praying, but, in truth, I would've already had my heart and my mind made up to not go.

"I don't feel like going. It's too much physical suffering," my flesh screamed out.

Fortunately, I actually did pray. I obeyed God. In turn, God blessed me. During my mission trips, I received the results of my scholarship. Now, I'm on a full ride scholarship for a masters in Contemporary Chinese Literature.

Below depicts the blessings of obedience:

> **Deuteronomy 28:1-14:** If you fully obey the Lord your God and carefully follow all his commands I give you today, the Lord your God will set you high above all the nations on earth. All these blessings will come on you and accompany you if you obey the Lord your God:

The Power of Esther and Ruth, God's Ordained Spouse for You

You will be blessed in the city and blessed in the country.
The fruit of your womb will be blessed, and the crops of your land and the young of your livestock—the calves of your herds and the lambs of your flocks.
Your basket and your kneading trough will be blessed.
You will be blessed when you come in and blessed when you go out.
The Lord will grant that the enemies who rise up against you will be defeated before you. They will come at you from one direction but flee from you in seven.
The Lord will send a blessing on your barns and on everything you put your hand to. The Lord your God will bless you in the land he is giving you.
The Lord will establish you as his holy people, as he promised you on oath, if you keep the commands of the Lord your God and walk in obedience to him. Then all the peoples on earth will see that you are called by the name of the Lord, and they will fear you. The Lord will grant you abundant prosperity—in the fruit of your womb, the young of your

livestock and the crops of your ground—in the land he swore to your ancestors to give you.

The Lord will open the heavens, the storehouse of his bounty, to send rain on your land in season and to bless all the work of your hands. You will lend to many nations but will borrow from none. The Lord will make you the head, not the tail. If you pay attention to the commands of the Lord your God that I give you this day and carefully follow them, you will always be at the top, never at the bottom. Do not turn aside from any of the commands I give you today, to the right or to the left, following other gods and serving them (NIV).

Arguably speaking, in this world, we will always war against our flesh and spirit.

Jeremiah 17:9: The heart is deceitful above all things and beyond cure. Who can understand it? (NIV).

Psalm 37:4: Take delight in the Lord,

and he will give you the desires of your heart (NIV).

A trauma survivor's biggest longing in life is for love, peace, joy (happiness), pleasure, and comfort. These desires are not wicked within themselves. In fact, God wants to give us love, peace, joy (happiness), pleasure, and comfort. The caveat is that it must be done God's way. God's way requires us to die to ourselves. The Bible promises that those who lose their life for His sake will gain it. Those who save their life will lose it (Matthew 16:25). The Kingdom's way is often the inverted form of the world's way. For this reason, God takes His daughters on a long and tedious process of untwisting us from this world's ideology and beliefs. As He renews and transforms our minds through His Word, we will truly know His good, perfect, and pleasing will.

Self-preservation and lack of trust often cripple the woman rising to be an overcomer. The brokenhearted woman starts off as a victim, turns into a survivor, and grows into a victorious overcomer. This is the stage that I am in now. I'm in between the hallways of surviving and overcoming. The root of my sin often stems from my lack of trust in God. When I do not trust God, I do not trust the people God places in my life. Thereby, I do not trust that the plans God has for me are good. In short, our desires within themselves are neutral. As we take delight in God, He will shape our hearts to desire His will above our own. The process of finding our authentic and true selves is hard, painful, and taxing. Yes, I admit. Many times, during this journey of healing, I almost threw in the towel and called it quits. It's only by the grace of God and His grace alone that I'm almost on the other side. Even then, I will never stop growing. We will always have room to grow until God calls us home. Sweet sister, I beseech you, DO NOT give up. If you have to come out on the other side looking busted, that is okay! One day, you will be a template for other women desiring true restoration and healing. That is, if you don't give up!

    Anytime you experience pain as a child, it is a temptation to identify any present painful and/or uncomfortable circumstance as abuse and injustice. This may or may not always be the case. Just because we went through hell as children, this doesn't mean we are entitled to pain-free lives as adults. We will face many trials and tribulations before we enter the Kingdom of God. Yes, nine out of ten times, our merciful God will not let us go through the same extent of pain that we had gone through as a child. Yet, pain is an indicator for us to identify what is really going on underneath our well put-together exteriors. Pain often reminds us that this world is NOT our home. Pain shakes us up, so we won't get comfortable and complacent. We need to grow up and face the pain head on. When we ignore, bury, and deny pain, we are only delaying our healing journey. Learn to face pain. Learn to embrace pain. Pain isn't always the enemy. Pain is used to develop Godly character within us. Pain drives us to do better and become better. The greatest women in history are often women who have a story to tell. These women overcame hell and high water. These women have gone through immense amounts of pain. In spite of it all, they did not allow past circumstances to define the present and future them. You are an overcomer! Don't stay on the floor forever, letting circumstances kick you to the ground over and over again. Stand up! I beseech you! Allow the pain that tunnels inside of your soul to make you better, not bitter.

Lastly, God prophetically spoke to our Apostle when he visited the East Asia branch. God usually speaks to me prophetically through food. That Sunday, our Apostle treated the whole congregation to several dishes at a Korean fusion restaurant. When it was my turn to look through the menu, I hesitated and flipped the pages for a long time. I glanced at sushi, but I thought to myself, "I'm not going to make him spend that much money." I skipped the sushi and I kept flipping the menu. He took the menu and picked a roll of salmon sushi for the sisters. This spoke to me prophetically because women get overwhelmed with choices. Sometimes, this means we aren't wise with all the decisions we make in respects to our choices with men. Secondly, Apostle didn't choose moldy food, food that had hair in it, food that had been rotting in the fridge for several days, or food that had come from the garbage truck. Often, trauma survivors believe the lie that God delights in torturing us, and anything is better than nothing. It was Satan, through our parents, who tortured us when we were small, not God. Yet, Apostle surprised the sisters with better than what we'd expected. Sushi suits me the best. It isn't disgusting looking. It doesn't look unappetizing like a soft-boiled fetal duck or balut, which is a delicacy that people from the Philippines eat. Nor, is it like a beautiful cake that has been badly burnt on the inside but covered with beautiful white frosting on the outside. Sushi, for me, represented something that was too expensive, so I didn't bother asking for it. It was something that I would have preferred, but it wasn't on the forefront of my mind. It was something I overlooked because of fear that I wasn't worthy. The salmon, on the other hand, exceeded all my expectations. God knows what we really need and He takes the deepest desires of our hearts into consideration.

> **1 Corinthians 2:9:** However, as it is written: "What no eye has seen, what no ear has heard, and what no human mind has conceived" -- the things God has prepared for those who love him (NIV).
>
> **Ephesians 3:20:** Now to him who is able to do immeasurably more than all

we ask or imagine, according to his power that is at work within us (NIV).

Perhaps your God-ordained husband is exceedingly better than what you have thought about in your imagination and your 'requirements' on your list that you formed when you were a broken woman. God has a good surprise for you! God doesn't want to torture, torment, and harm you. Whenever you are afraid that a particular person is going to ask you out, it's because that is a familiar spirit. You are running from that spirit that was/or is inside of you. Do not fear, God has someone who suits you well and who you will like, too!

Luke 11:11-13: "Which of you fathers, if your son asks for a fish, will give him a snake instead? Or if he asks for an egg, will give him a scorpion? If you then, though you are evil, know how to give good gifts to your children, how much more will your Father in heaven give the Holy Spirit to those who ask him (NIV).

Chapter 13

After Healing: The Proverbs 31 Woman

I used to believe that marriage would mean the end of my life, as most women would believe that marriage would be the beginning of their lives. I believed that once I was married, I could just rely on the man and lose myself in him. I wouldn't have to work so hard. I've since learned that this is the very definition of codependency. That was what my mother attempted to do with my father. As I grieved my losses, the adult who wants to take responsibility and make commitments has begun to emerge. I learned to forgive my parents and let them go, because they did the best they could with the emotional, mental, and financial resources they possessed at the time. Whenever the bitterness does rise up, I quickly wrestle it down, and I pray for their prosperity and repentance. After all, you can only give what you have. Now, I realize that God allowed Satan to sift me like wheat, because God trained my hands for spiritual warfare at a young age. I am able to use what I learned in my life to set other young women free.

> God doesn't give you the people you want, but the people you need to help you, hurt you, lead you, love you, leave you, to make you into the person you were meant to be!
> ~Apostle Joseph Min

The Bible says it this way,
> **Isaiah 61:1-4:** The Spirit of the Sovereign Lord is on me, because the Lord has anointed me to <u>preach good news to the poor</u>. He has <u>sent me to bind up the brokenhearted</u>, to <u>proclaim freedom for the captives</u> and <u>release from darkness</u> for the prisoners, and <u>proclaim the year of the Lord's favor</u> and the <u>day of vengeance</u> of our God, to <u>comfort all who mourn</u>. And <u>provide for those who grieve</u> in Zion to bestow on <u>them a crown of beauty</u> instead of ashes, <u>the oil of gladness</u> instead of mourning, <u>and a garment of praise</u>

instead of a spirit of despair. They will be called oaks of righteousness, a planting of the Lord for the display of his splendor. They will <u>rebuild the ancient ruins and restore the places long devastated</u>; they will <u>renew the ruined cities</u> that have been <u>devastated for **generations**</u>.

The anointing on our lives is to preach the good news to the poor in spirit, bind up the wounds of the brokenhearted, bring deliverance to the captives, and set people who are in bondage free. We are supposed to bring the oil of gladness to generations who have been mourning. We will restore and rebuild what has been stolen from people of previous generations.

In conclusion, romance and becoming a wife will not make the sting of sadness cease, since trauma survivors have lost their entire childhoods. It's only God who will heal that sting of sadness in His timing. Our peace and joy in life comes from the Holy Spirit's leading. Marriage is not a place for young women to be lazy, play, and have fun. That's what is potentially found in singleness. Marriage is ministry. Marriage is hard work. Fortunately, the Bible promises us that what Satan has stolen from us, God will restore it seven-fold.

> **Proverbs 6:30-31:** *Men* do not despise a thief, if he steal to satisfy his soul when he is hungry; But *if* he be found, <u>he shall restore sevenfold</u>; he shall give all the substance of his house (KJV).

Satan has stolen a lot from your family and the previous generations. Now, that he is caught, he has to pay and suffer for the rest of his life. The blessings are in your hands now. Reach for your healing and God will restore to you all that the locusts have eaten.

A healthy husband and wife duo is found in the example of the Proverbs 31 woman.

> **Proverbs 31:10-31 (MSG):** A good woman is hard to find, and worth far more than diamonds.
> Her husband trusts her without reserve, and never has reason to regret it.
> Never spiteful, she treats him generously all her life long.

After Healing: The Proverbs 31 Woman

She shops around for the best yarns and cottons, and enjoys knitting and sewing.
She's like a trading ship that sails to faraway places and brings back exotic surprises.
She's up before dawn, preparing breakfast for her family and organizing her day.
She looks over a field and buys it, then, with money she's put aside, plants a garden.
First thing in the morning, she dresses for work, rolls up her sleeves, eager to get started.
She senses the worth of her work, is in no hurry to call it quits for the day.
She's skilled in the crafts of home and hearth, diligent in homemaking.
She's quick to assist anyone in need, reaches out to help the poor.
She doesn't worry about her family when it snows; their winter clothes are all mended and ready to wear.
She makes her own clothing, and dresses in colorful linens and silks.
Her husband is greatly respected when he deliberates with the city fathers.

She designs gowns and sells them, brings the sweaters she knits to the dress shops.
Her clothes are well-made and elegant, and she always faces tomorrow with a smile.
When she speaks she has something worthwhile to say, and she always says it kindly.
She keeps an eye on everyone in her household, and keeps them all busy and productive.
Her children respect and bless her; her husband joins in with words of praise:
"Many women have done wonderful things, but you've outclassed them all!"
Charm can mislead and beauty soon fades. The woman to be admired and praised is the woman who lives in the Fear-of-God.
Give her everything she deserves! Festoon her life with praises!

The Proverbs 31 woman marries a very successful man. She marries a husband with a good name, because he is greatly respected. This man deals with the top leaders, so he is prominent and affluent. He is a very powerful man. Yet, the story doesn't stop here. The woman has goals, purpose, and a life outside of her husband and children. She has an identity outside of the people she is connected to. She is aware of her internal value, as she is worth diamonds. She has good character, because she is trustworthy. She runs a business on the side because she looks at land, buys the land, and produces from the land. She also runs a clothing business. Her hobbies are to knit and sew. She is self-sufficient, and is able to make her own clothes with colorful linens and silks. She takes care of herself and dresses presentably. In order to maintain her household and all her external responsibilities, she rises up before dawn, preparing food for her family. Her children respect her because she is a good mother. She is a good steward of her time and talents. She is a good leader, because she is able to divide responsibility. Her words are full of tact, and she has a tight reign on her tongue. She is prepared for the future, because she prepares her children's winter clothes. She has ministry outside the home, because she helps the poor. She's perseverant, kind, intelligent, wise, educated, tactful, crafty, and much more.

These are just some facts I have gleaned from the text.

Has God prepared you to be this kind of wife? Sister, I beseech you, if you are not the Proverbs 31 woman, you aren't ready to be a wife yet. Otherwise, you will marry a bum in a pothole. You attract who you are. Don't marry a man who will bring generational curses to the next generation. You have already overcome so much! Stand tall, sister! God's got you!

Bibliography

"11 Facts About Child Abuse." *DoSomething.org*, www.dosomething.org/us/facts/11-facts-about-child-abuse#:~:text=Approximately%205%20children%20die%20every,the%20perpetrator%20in%20some%20way.

American Psychological Association, American Psychological Association, www.apa.org/topics/trauma/.

Aponte, Catherine. "Do Women Really Talk More Than Men?" *Psychology Today*, Sussex Publishers, 10 Oct. 2019, www.psychologytoday.com/us/blog/marriage-equals/201910/do-women-really-talk-more-men.

Blue Letter Bible, www.blueletterbible.org/.

Boom, Corrie Ten. *The Hiding Place*. Hendrickson Publishers, 2015.

Bradshaw, John. *Healing the Shame That Binds You*. HEALTH COMMUNICATIONS, 2015.

Demuth, Mary. *Not Marked (4 X 6): Finding Hope and Healing After Sexual Abuse*. CreateSpace Independent Publishing Platform; 1 Edition, 2015.

Elliot, Elisabeth. *Passion and Purity: Learning to Bring Your Love Life under Christ's Control*.

Revell, a Division of Baker Publishing Group, 2013.

Gao, Helen. "A Scar on the Chinese Soul." 18 Jan. 2017.

Holland, Kimberly. "Stockholm Syndrome: Causes, Symptoms, Examples." *Healthline*, Healthline Media, 11 Nov. 2019, www.healthline.com/health/mental-health/stockholm-syndrome#:~:text=What%20is%20Stockholm%20syndrome%3F,years%20of%20captivity%20or%20abuse.

Lancer, Darlene. "Sibling Bullying and Abuse: The Hidden Epidemic." *Psychology Today*, Sussex Publishers, 3 Feb. 2020, www.psychologytoday.com/us/blog/toxic-relationships/202002/sibling-bullying-and-abuse-the-hidden-epidemic.

Lancer, Darlene. "Sibling Bullying and Abuse: The Hidden Epidemic." *Psychology Today*, Sussex Publishers, 3 Feb. 2020, www.psychologytoday.com/us/blog/toxic-relationships/202002/sibling-bullying-and-abuse-the-hidden-epidemic.

Learning, Lumen. "Introduction to Psychology." *Lumen*, courses.lumenlearning.com/wmopen-psychology/chapter/prosocial-behavior/.

Lee, Rebecca. "Emotional Incest: When Is Close Too Close?" *World of Psychology*, 8 July

2018, psychcentral.com/blog/emotional-incest-when-is-close-too-close/.

Lehrner A, Yehuda R. Cultural trauma and epigenetic inheritance. Dev Psychopathol. 2018;30(5):1763-1777. doi:10.1017/S0954579418001153

"Marriage and Divorce." *American Psychological Association*, American Psychological Association, www.apa.org/topics/divorce/.

Miller, Alice. *The Drama of the Gifted Child: The Search for the True Self*. 1979.

Murray, Sarah Hunter. "How Often Should Couples Have Sex?" *Psychology Today*, Sussex Publishers, 25 Sept. 2018, www.psychologytoday.com/us/blog/myths-desire/201809/how-often-should-couples-have-sex#:~:text=The%20researchers%20concluded%20that%20couples,having%20sex%20once%20a%20week.

"Oxford Learner's Dictionaries: Find Definitions, Translations, and Grammar Explanations at Oxford Learner's Dictionaries." *Oxford Learner's Dictionaries | Find Definitions, Translations, and Grammar Explanations at Oxford Learner's Dictionaries*, www.oxfordlearnersdictionaries.com/.

"Read & Study The Bible - Daily Verse, Scripture by Topic, Stories." *Bible Study Tools*, www.biblestudytools.com/.

Walker, Pete. "The 4Fs: A Trauma Typology in Complex PTSD By Pete Walker." *Pete Walker, M.A. Psychotherapy*, pete-walker.com/fourFs_TraumaTypologyComplexPTSD.htm#:~:text=The%204Fs%3A%20A%20Trauma%20Typology,By%20Pete%20Walker&text=This%20model%20elaborates%20four%20basic,referred%20to%20as%20the%204Fs).

Washington, Department. "Sexual Behaviour and Children ." *Department of Washington State* , depts.washington.edu/hcsats/PDF/TF-%20CBT/pages/3%20Psychoeducation/Child%20Sexual%20Behaviors/Sexual%20Behavior%20and%20Children.pdf.

"Why Breeding Your Dog on Her First Heat Is Not OK." Pet Parents® - Healthy Pets. Happy Family.®, petparentsbrand.com/blogs/petblog/why-breeding-your-dog-on-her-first-heat-is-not-ok.

About the Author

Jessica King loves a good story. She believes that God is the best storyteller. As a master's student and avid traveler, she enjoys learning and dabbling into new realms of knowledge. She hopes to be able to learn Japanese one day and start a skincare line.